Money and Asset Prices in Boom and Bust

Money and Asset Prices in Boom and Bust

TIM CONGDON

The Institute of Economic Affairs

First published in Great Britain in 2005 by
The Institute of Economic Affairs
2 Lord North Street
Westminster
London SW1P 3LB
in association with Profile Books Ltd

The mission of the Institute of Economic Affairs is to improve public understanding of the fundamental institutions of a free society, with particular reference to the role of markets in solving economic and social problems.

A CIP catalogue record for this book is available from the British Library.

ISBN 0 255 36570 5

Many IEA publications are translated into languages other than English or are reprinted. Permission to translate or to reprint should be sought from the Director General at the address above.

Typeset in Stone by MacGuru Ltd
info@macguru.org.uk
Printed and bound in Great Britain by Hobbs the Printers

CONTENTS

THE AUTHOR

Professor Tim Congdon is one of Britain's leading economic commentators. He was a member of the Treasury Panel of Independent Forecasters (the so-called 'wise men'), which advised the Chancellor of the Exchequer on economic policy, between 1992 and 1997. He founded Lombard Street Research, the City of London's leading economic research and forecasting consultancy, in 1989, and is its Chief Economist. He has been a visiting professor at the Cardiff Business School and the City University Business School (now the Sir John Cass Business School). He has written a number of books on monetary policy, contributes widely to the financial press, and makes frequent radio and television appearances. He writes a column in the Institute of Economic Affairs journal, *Economic Affairs*. He was awarded the CBE for services to economic debate in 1997.

FOREWORD

The Institute of Economic Affairs was at the forefront of promoting a wider understanding of the relationship between the money supply and inflation at a time when virtually the whole of the British economics profession was either sceptical or hostile to monetarism. Eventually, the IEA succeeded in educating a generation of economists, commentators, opinion formers and policymakers. Now it is widely believed not only that inflation is a monetary phenomenon, but that output and employment cannot be expanded, in anything other than the short term, by loosening monetary policy. The decision to make the Bank of England operationally independent, in May 1997, perhaps suggests that the IEA's work in this field is complete.

But to take this view would be to exhibit a reckless degree of complacency, for two reasons. The first is because fashions in economic opinion can change if correct and rigorous theories are not updated and explained in terms relevant to changed times. The second is because, while the basic, underlying, long-term relationship between money and inflation is widely accepted, many aspects of monetary policy are not well understood. Arguably, it is for this reason, among others, that inflation did not fall smoothly from the high levels of the 1970s to the lower levels of today, and it is also for this reason that there were booms and busts in asset prices and the real economy during the intervening 30 years.

In Hobart Paper 152, Tim Congdon argues that, on many occasions in the last 30 years, policy-makers have taken their eyes off money supply growth. As a result, we have suffered booms and busts in asset prices and lapses in our record of reducing and then controlling inflation. Congdon looks at several episodes in history, such as the Great Depression in the USA, the bubble of the late 1980s in Japan and the subsequent malaise of weak demand in the 1990s, and the Heath–Barber boom of the early 1970s in Britain. He concludes that in every case the underlying cause was a large fluctuation in the growth rate of the money supply, broadly defined to include all bank deposits. When broad money growth is too rapid, excess money leads to asset price gains and buoyant demand, and ultimately to inflation. On the other hand, when broad money growth slows too abruptly (and particularly when broad money contracts), asset prices and demand weaken, and in due course inflation moderates or is replaced by deflation.

Despite the widespread acceptance of the monetary explanation of inflation in general terms, the details of the transmission mechanism from money to the economy remain controversial. Congdon argues that in the UK poor understanding of the transmission mechanism was responsible for mistakes in monetary policy in the late 1980s (in the so-called 'Lawson boom'). These mistakes were similar to those in the Heath–Barber boom of the early 1970s. Largely because of violent swings in money supply growth, an asset price boom and subsequent inflation were followed by a slump in asset prices and a recession.

It is tempting to dismiss ideas about the relationship between the money supply and the economy as issues that should be discussed mainly by central bank technocrats and academics, as technical matters relevant only to those involved with the minutiae of monetary policy in a world where most people are persuaded that inflation is a monetary phenomenon. To do so would be very dangerous. Congdon's message is relevant to financial institutions that are making forecasts about the future direction of equity and bond markets. It is relevant to individuals trying to deal with 'ups and downs' in housing markets. Most of all, if Congdon is right, and if his message is not understood by policy-makers, there will be surges and slumps in inflation as we have continually to relearn the lesson that money matters. Indeed, many argue that at least the scale of the Conservatives' last three election defeats, if not their fact, can be explained by the mismanagement of the economy between 1985 and 1992. Congdon argues that the dramatic increase in broad money growth in the late 1980s and the plunge in broad money growth in the early 1990s, which reflected mistakes in monetary policy, were the main causes of the boom–bust cycle. If the boom–bust cycle had been avoided, our recent political history might have looked rather different.

Thus the issues raised in Hobart Paper 152 are of profound importance, not just to those involved with directing and commenting on economic policy, but also to a wider public, including those working in financial markets and those who wish to understand recent political history.

The views expressed in this Hobart Paper are, as in all IEA publications, those of the author and not those of the Institute (which has no corporate view), its managing trustees, Academic Advisory Council members or senior staff.

PHILIP BOOTH

Editorial and Programme Director, Institute of Economic Affairs,
Professor of Insurance and Risk Management,
Sir John Cass Business School, City University

July 2005

SUMMARY

- While most economists today accept that inflation is a
  monetary phenomenon, there is still much dispute about
  the mechanism of transmission from monetary policy to
  inflation and about the significance of different measures of
  the quantity of money.
- These areas of dispute are extremely important in policy-
  making. If appropriate measures of the money supply are not
  monitored and controlled, serious episodes of 'boom and
  bust' will arise.
- In the USA and to some extent the UK the quantity of broad
  money has been neglected in setting monetary policy in the
  last few years. Interest rates have been regarded not just as
  the main or even the only instrument of monetary policy, but
  as defining the stance of monetary policy.
- Fluctuations in the growth rate of broad money played a
  causal role in:
  - the UK's boom–bust cycles of the 1970s and 1980s (i.e.
    the Heath–Barber boom and subsequent bust of the
    early 1970s, and the Lawson boom and ensuing recession
    between 1985 and 1992);
  - the US's Great Depression in the early 1930s; and
  - the Japanese bubble in the 1980s and the macroeconomic
    malaise of the 1990s.

- In the upswing phase of the Heath–Barber boom and the Lawson boom, the broad money holdings of non-bank financial institutions rose explosively. This led directly to an asset price boom as institutions tried to adjust their money balances to the desired proportion of their total portfolios.
- The US's Great Depression was accompanied by a collapse in broad money and the Japanese asset price malaise of the 1990s by stagnation in broad money.
- Because of the link between assets and goods markets, asset price booms play a major part in the development of general inflation that inevitably follows a period of lax broad money growth.
- Causality runs from money to asset prices and inflation, not the other way round. In an analysis of the mechanisms at work it becomes clear that the quantity of broad money, but not of narrow money, can cause financial institutions and companies to change their behaviour. In fact, the narrow money holdings of companies and financial institutions are insignificant.
- Theories that relate asset price booms to the volume of credit, or to bank lending, rather than to the quantity of money are misconceived.
- The key variable for understanding and controlling periods of boom and bust is the growth of broad money. The behaviour of the quantity of broad money will remain fundamental to understanding the behaviour of asset prices and the general price level in market economies in the future.

TABLES AND FIGURES

AUTHOR'S PREFACE

The themes of this paper have been with me for my 35 years as an economist, first as a student and then as a practitioner in the City of London and a visiting professor at two business schools. The paper's central message is simple and has always seemed obvious to me. It is that fluctuations in asset prices and economic activity must be related to, and can be largely explained by, more or less contemporaneous fluctuations in a broadly defined, all-inclusive measure of money. But aspects of the analysis are quite complex and have over the years generated immense controversy, particularly my insistence that only a broadly defined aggregate can be relevant to the determination of asset prices (and so of national income). As the controversies have sharpened my thinking, I would like to thank a number of people for their contribution to its development.

I first applied a naive theoretical understanding of monetary economics to the day-to-day reporting and interpretation of events as a journalist on *The Times* between 1973 and 1976, and am hugely grateful to Peter Jay, then the economics editor, and William Rees-Mogg (now Lord Rees-Mogg), then the editor, for their interest in my work. I developed parts of the argument as one of the economics partners of the stockbroker firm L. Messel & Co., and benefited from collaboration with Paul Turnbull, particularly in the introduction of the concept of 'mortgage equity withdrawal'. In the late 1970s I got to know Terry Burns (now Lord Burns) and Alan (now Sir Alan) Budd at the London Business School, and we usefully discussed the impact of excess money on the prices of foreign goods and assets via the exchange rate. Later Dr Peter Warburton worked with me in creating a small econometric model of the UK economy incorporating monetary variables. Together we forecast the main features of the 'Lawson boom' in 1987 and 1988, when virtually all other forecasting groups were hopelessly wrong. I founded a company, Lombard Street Research, in 1989 to analyse the relationships between money and the economy in greater depth. I was lucky there to have the support both of numerous clients and of several excellent colleagues, and I would particularly like to mention Simon Ward and Stewart Robertson. Simon and Stewart carried out most of the difficult back-room work on the Lombard Street Research model, and I am most grateful to them. The current chairman of Lombard Street Research, Professor Gordon Pepper, has challenged and improved my thinking, and again I must say 'thank you'. Much of the work in this paper was carried out while I was engaged in a more ambitious research project at Cardiff Business School. Richard Wild, now of the Office of National Statistics, was my research assistant at Cardiff and helped me by preparing an index of asset prices, and again: 'thank you'. I am also much obliged to my editor at the IEA, Professor Philip Booth, who asked some good questions, kept the study under control and made necessary changes.

Over the years I have benefited from considerable interaction with academic economists. Professor Vicky Chick, Dr Walter Eltis, Professor Charles Goodhart and Professor David Laidler have commented on my pieces with sympathetic criticism, and I owe them a great deal. Professor Allan Meltzer disagrees with the main thesis of this paper, but I greatly valued his thoughts on it. Finally, may I say that some of the best criticism of my work in the last two years has come from Milton Friedman? He has taken time and trouble to find weak links in the argument, and to point them out to me. My debt to him both for this, and as the background inspiration for much of my work for over 30 years, will be obvious from the paper itself. However, my emphasis on the role of *broad* money in the determination of asset prices, and on the rather chaotic and highly institutional nature of the processes at work, now seems to me more Keynesian than monetarist in spirit. In effect the whole paper is an analysis of the empirical significance of the speculative demand for money. But in one respect Keynes was wrong and Friedman right. In the real world instability in the *supply* of money is a far more important cause of macroeconomic turbulence than instability in the *demand* for money.

Of course, I alone am responsible for the contents of the paper and its remaining mistakes.

Money and Asset Prices in Boom and Bust

1 MONEY AND EXPENDITURE IN THE TRANSMISSION MECHANISM

How does money influence the economy? More exactly, how do changes in the level (or the rate of growth) of the quantity of money affect the values of key macroeconomic variables such as aggregate demand and the price level? As these are straightforward questions which have been asked for over four hundred years, economic theory ought by now to have given some reasonably definitive answers. But that is far from being the case.

Most economists agree with the proposition that in the long run inflation is 'a monetary phenomenon', in the sense that it is associated with faster increases in the quantity of money than in the quantity of goods and services produced. But they disagree about almost everything else in monetary economics, with particular uncertainty about the so-called 'transmission mechanism'. The purpose of this monograph is to describe key aspects of the transmission mechanism from money, on the one hand, to asset prices and economic activity, on the other, in advanced industrial economies with large financial markets. The experience of the UK economy in the business cycles from the 1960s to today will be considered in most detail, with particular emphasis on the two pronounced boom–bust cycles in the early 1970s and the late 1980s. But two other episodes – the Great Depression in the USA from 1929 to 1933 and the prolonged malaise in the Japanese economy in the decade or so from 1992 – will also be discussed.

A central theme will be the importance of the quantity of money, broadly defined to include nearly all bank deposits, in asset price determination. Narrow money measures are shown to be almost irrelevant to asset price determination in a modern economy. One chapter will rebut claims that 'credit' is relevant, *by itself*, to asset price determination and economic activity; it will argue that such claims, which have become surprisingly common in professional journals and central bank bulletins in recent years, are confused and misleading. In order better to locate the analysis in the wider debates, a discussion of the origins of certain key motivating ideas is necessary.

Traditional accounts of the transmission mechanism

Irving Fisher of the University of Yale was the first economist to set out, with rigorous statistical techniques, the facts of the relationship between money and the price level in his 1911 study, *The Purchasing Power of Money*. Fisher's aim was to revive and defend the quantity theory of money. In his review of Fisher's book for the *Economic Journal*, John Maynard Keynes was mostly friendly, but expressed some reservations. In his words, 'The most serious defect in Professor Fisher's doctrine is to be found in his account of the mode by which through transitional stages an influx of new money affects prices.'[1] In the preface to the second edition, Fisher summarised Keynes's criticism as being the claim that, although his 'book shows *that* changes in the quantity of money do affect

---

1   Elizabeth Johnson and Donald Moggridge (eds), *The Collected Writings of John Maynard Keynes*, vol. XI, *Economic Articles and Correspondence* (London and Basingstoke: Macmillan Press for the Royal Economic Society, 1983), p. 376.

the price level', it 'does not show *how* they do so'.[2] In other words, Keynes felt that Fisher had not provided a satisfactory version of the transmission mechanism.

Fisher quickly responded to Keynes. In fact, he used the opportunity of the preface to the second edition of *The Purchasing Power of Money* to direct Keynes to pages 242–7 of another of his works, *Elementary Principles of Economics*, which had been published in 1912 between the first and second editions of *The Purchasing Power*. In those pages, entitled 'An increase in money does not decrease its velocity', Fisher noted that economic agents have a desired ratio of money to expenditure determined by 'habit' and 'convenience'. If 'some mysterious Santa Claus suddenly doubles the amount [of money] in the possession of each individual', economic agents have excess money balances. They try to get rid of their excess money by increasing their purchases in the shops, leading to 'a sudden briskness in trade', rising prices and depleting stocks. It might appear that only a few days of high spending should enable people to reduce their money balances to the desired level, but 'we must not forget that the only way in which the individual can get rid of his money is by handing it over to somebody else. Society is not rid of it'. To put it another way, the payments are being made within a closed circuit. It follows that, under Fisher's 'Santa Claus hypothesis', the shopkeepers who receive the surplus cash 'will, in their turn, endeavour to get rid of it by purchasing goods for their business'. Therefore, 'the effort to get rid of it and the consequent effect on prices will continue until prices have reached a sufficiently high level'. The 'sufficiently high level' is attained

---

2   William J. Barber (ed.), *The Works of Irving Fisher*, vol. 4, *The Purchasing Power of Money* (London: Pickering & Chatto, 1997, originally published by Macmillan, New York, 1911), p. 27.

when prices and expenditure have risen so much that the original desired ratio of money to expenditure has been restored. Prices, as well as the quantity of money, will have doubled.[3]

Three features of Fisher's statement of the transmission mechanism in his *Elementary Principles of Economics* are:

- the emphasis on the stability of the desired ratio of money to expenditure;
- the distinction between 'the individual experiment' (in which every money-holder tries to restore his own desired money/expenditure ratio, given the price level, by changing his money balances) and 'the market experiment' (in which, with the quantity of money held by all individuals being given and hence invariant to the efforts of the individuals to change it, the price level must adjust to take them back to their desired money/expenditure ratios); and
- the lack of references to 'the interest rate' in agents' adjustments of their expenditure to their money holdings.[4]

These are also the hallmarks of several subsequent descriptions of the transmission mechanism. In 1959 Milton Friedman – who became the leading exponent of the quantity theory in the

---

3   Barber (ed.), *Works of Fisher*, vol. 5, *Elementary Principles of Economics* (London: Pickering & Chatto, 1997, originally published by Macmillan, New York, 1912), pp. 242–4.

4   The analysis on pp. 242–7 of *Elementary Principles* is different from that in Chapter 4 of *Purchasing Power*, even though Chapter 4 had ostensibly been on the same subject of 'the transition period' (i.e. the passage of events in the transmission mechanism). Chapter 4 of *Purchasing Power* is highly Wicksellian, with much discussion of the relationship between interest rates and the rate of price change, and then between real interest rates and credit demands. This Wicksellian strand was dropped in pp. 242–7 of *Elementary Principles*.

1960s and 1970s – made a statement to the US Congress about the relationship between money and the economy. He recalled Fisher's themes. After emphasising the stability of agents' preferences for money, he noted that 'if individuals as a whole were to try to reduce the number of dollars they held, they could not all do so, they would simply be playing a game of musical chairs'. In response to a sudden increase in the quantity of money, expenditure decisions would keep on being revised until the right balance between money and incomes had returned. While individuals may be 'frustrated in their attempt to reduce the number of dollars they hold, they succeed in achieving an equivalent change in their position, for the rise in money income and in prices reduces the ratio of these balances to their income and also the real value of these balances'.[5] Friedman has also emphasised throughout his career the superiority of monetary aggregates over interest rates as measures of monetary policy.

The claim that, in a long-run equilibrium, the real value of agents' money balances would not be altered by changes in the nominal quantity of money was also a central contention of Patinkin's *Money, Interest and Prices*, the first edition of which was published in 1955. *Money, Interest and Prices* exploited the distinction between the individual and market experiments in a detailed theoretical elaboration of what Patinkin termed 'the real-balance effect'. In his view 'a real-balance effect in the commodity markets is the *sine qua non* of monetary theory'.[6] The real-balance effect

---

5   See Milton Friedman, 'Statement on monetary theory and policy', given in congressional hearings in 1959, reprinted on pp. 136–45 of R. James Ball and Peter Boyle (eds), *Inflation* (Harmondsworth: Penguin, 1969). The quotations are from p. 141.

6   Donald Patinkin, *Money, Interest and Prices* (New York: Harper & Row, 2nd edn, 1965), p. 21. Keynes is sometimes said to be the originator of the idea of 'real

can be viewed as the heart of the transmission mechanism from money to the economy. The real balance effect is discussed further in the Appendix (page 139).

Asset prices in the traditional accounts

Despite the lucidity of their descriptions of the transmission mechanism, the impact of Fisher, Friedman and Patinkin on the discussion of macroeconomic policy in the final 40 years of the twentieth century was mixed. In the 1970s Friedman had great success in persuading governments and central banks that curbing the growth of the money supply was vital if they wanted to reduce inflation. His theoretical work on money was contested, however, by other leading economists and did not command universal acceptance. By the 1990s the preponderance of academic work on monetary policy focused on interest rates, with the relationship between interest rates and the components of demand in a Keynesian income-expenditure model attracting most attention.[7] For example, when it was asked in 1999 by the Treasury

balances', as he used the general idea in his 1923 book *A Tract on Monetary Reform* in a discussion of inflation in revolutionary Russia in the early 1920s. Patinkin's view on the importance of the real-balance effect seems to have changed in his later years. In an entry on 'Real balances' in the 1987 *Palgrave* he said: 'the significance of the real-balance effect is in the realm of macroeconomic theory and not policy'. (See John Eatwell et al. [eds], *The New Palgrave: Money* [London and Basingstoke: Macmillan, 1989, based on 1987 *New Palgrave*], p. 307.) See also the Appendix to this text.

7   In the autumn of 1995 *The Journal of Economic Perspectives* published a number of papers on the transmission mechanism of monetary policy. Not one of the papers focused on the real-balance effect as the heart of this mechanism. Indeed, despite Fisher's and Friedman's clear statements many years earlier, and Friedman's and many others' vast output on the empirical relationship between money and the economy, Bernanke and Gertler opined that 'empirical analysis of the effects of

Committee of the House of Commons for its views on the transmission mechanism, the Bank of England prepared a paper in which 'official rates' (i.e. short-term interest rates under the Bank's control) influenced 'market rates', asset prices, expectations and confidence, and the exchange rate, and these four variables then impacted on domestic demand and net external demand. In a twelve-page note it reached page ten before acknowledging that 'we have discussed how monetary policy changes affect output and inflation, with barely a mention of the quantity of money'.[8] The links between money, in the sense of 'the quantity of money', and the economy were widely neglected or even forgotten.

The relatively simple accounts of the transmission mechanism in Fisher's *Purchasing Power of Money* and some of Friedman's popular work were particularly vulnerable on one score. They concentrated on the relationship between money and expenditure on the goods and services that constitute national income, but neglected the role of financial assets and capital goods in the economy; they analysed the work that money performs in the *flow* of income and expenditure, but did not say how it fits into the numerous individual portfolios that represent a society's *stock* of capital assets. As Keynes had highlighted in his *Treatise on Money*

---

monetary policy has treated the monetary transmission mechanism as a "black box"' (Ben Bernanke and Mark Gertler, 'Inside the black box: the credit channel of monetary policy transmission', *Journal of Economic Perspectives* [Minneapolis: American Economic Association, 1995], pp. 27–48. The quotation is from p. 27).

8   The Monetary Policy Committee of the Bank of England, *The transmission mechanism of monetary policy* (London: Bank of England, in response to suggestions by the Treasury Committee of the House of Commons, 1999), p. 10. The note is believed to have been written by John Vickers, the Bank's chief economist at the time. See also Spencer Dale and Andrew G. Haldane, 'Interest rates and the channels of monetary transmission: some sectoral estimates' (London: Bank of England, Working Paper Series no. 18, 1993), for a description of the transmission mechanism in which the quantity of money plays no motivating role.

(published in 1931), money is used in two classes of transaction – those in goods, services and tangible capital assets (or 'the industrial circulation', as he called it), and those in financial assets ('the financial circulation').[9] The need was therefore to refurbish monetary theory, so that money was located in an economy with capital assets and could affect asset prices as well as the price level of goods and services. Much of Friedman's theoretical work for a professional audience was a response to this requirement. For example, in a 1964 paper written with Meiselman he contrasted a 'credit' view, in which monetary policy 'impinges on a narrow and well-defined range of capital assets and a correspondingly narrow range of associated expenditures', with a 'monetary' view, in which it 'impinges on a much broader range of capital assets and correspondingly broader range of associated expenditures'.[10]

But most macroeconomists have remained more comfortable

---

9   Johnson and Moggridge (eds), *Collected Writings of Keynes*, vol. V, *A Treatise on Money: The Pure Theory of Money* (London and Basingstoke: Macmillan Press for the Royal Economic Society, 1971, originally published 1930), ch. 15, 'The industrial circulation and the financial circulation', pp. 217–30. Keynes argued that 'the industrial circulation … will vary with … the aggregate of money incomes, i.e., with the volume and cost of production of current output' (p. 221), whereas 'the financial circulation is … determined by quite a different set of considerations' (p. 222). In his words, 'the amount of business deposits … required to look after financial business depends – apart from possible variations in the velocity of these deposits – on the volume of trading × the average value of the instruments traded' (also p. 222). Arguably, these remarks contained the germ of the later distinction between the transactions and speculative motives for holding money. In the discussion of the financial circulation in *A Treatise of Money*, securities (i.e. equities and bonds) are the alternative to money; in the discussion of the speculative demand to hold money in *The General Theory* bonds are the alternative to money.

10   Friedman and David Meiselman, 'The relative stability of monetary velocity and the investment multiplier in the United States, 1897–1958', in *Stabilization Policies* (Englewood Cliffs, N J: Prentice Hall for the Commission on Money and Credit,1963), pp. 165–268. See, in particular, p. 217.

with the notion that interest rates affect investment (and, at a further remove, the level of national income) than with the claim that the quantity of money has an empirically significant and verifiable role in asset price determination (and that asset prices are fundamental to cyclical fluctuations in national income). The purpose of this study is to challenge the dominant view; it is to show that money was crucial to asset price fluctuations in the UK in the last four decades of the twentieth century, in the USA during the Great Depression and in Japan in the decade or so leading up to the 21st century.

The next chapter will present a monetary account of asset price determination, set in a UK context. It will abstract from institutional complexities in order to convey the essence of the processes at work; it will appeal to the first two of the three distinctive features of the naive transmission mechanism discussed by Fisher in 1912 and Friedman in his 1959 congressional testimony, namely the stability of the relevant agents' demand for money and the need to differentiate between the individual and market experiments; and it will argue that these ideas are useful in the context of the financial markets where asset prices are set, just as they are in the markets for the goods and services which enter consumer price indices. Of course, the real world is a complicated place, and agents' preferences for money and other assets may change radically in a world of extreme asset price turbulence. Even so, Chapters 3 and 4 will contain a discussion of the asset price experiences of three nations widely separated in space and time, and will demonstrate the relevance to all of them of the analytical approach adopted here.

2 MONEY AND ASSET PRICES IN THE TRANSMISSION MECHANISM

Before relating money to asset prices, some remarks on the structure of wealth and ownership patterns are necessary. The focus here will be on the UK, since the UK had particularly severe asset price and macroeconomic instability in the late twentieth century, and receives most attention in this paper. Ample official data on the UK's wealth are available. The main constituents of the capital stock throughout the 40 years were residential houses, land and infrastructure, commercial property, and plant and equipment (including ships, planes and cars). Roughly speaking, the value of the assets was five times that of national income. In the final analysis all these assets were owned by people. But often they were registered in the names of companies and financial institutions, and people owned claims on the companies in the form of directly held equities or bonds, and they owned claims on the financial institutions by such means as insurance policies or unit trusts. For a variety of motives – for example, to achieve diversity in their asset portfolios, to enjoy the advantages of specialised investment management and to exploit favourable tax treatment – many households built up their assets through long-term savings products marketed by financial institutions.

Because of these patterns, the twentieth century saw a rise in the proportion of corporate equity quoted on the stock exchange in tandem with the institutionalisation of saving. As shown by

Table 1 **Beneficial ownership of UK shares, 1963–89**

	1963	1975	1989
Insurance companies	10.0	15.9	18.6
Pension funds	6.4	16.8	30.6
Unit trusts	1.3	4.1	5.9
Investment trusts and other OFIs	11.3	10.5	2.7
Total institutional	29.0	47.3	57.8

Source: *Economic Trends*, January 1991 issue, article on 'The 1989 Share Register Survey'

Table 1, financial institutions became the principal holders of UK quoted equities in the closing decades of the century.[1] They also held substantial portfolios of commercial property and other assets, such as government and corporate bonds.

Indeed, over most of the 40 years to the end of the century the institutions were so large that their activities were crucial in the determination of asset prices and particularly of share prices. In the USA and Japan financial institutions also played a major role in asset price setting in the twentieth century, although a higher proportion of equities were registered in the hands of persons (so-called 'retail investors') than in the UK. A key question arises from the institutions' heavyweight role in asset markets. What was the significance of money in their portfolio decisions? Is it sensible to view their attitudes towards their holdings of equities, and other assets, as being powerfully influenced by their money balances or not?

---

1   Ted Doggett, 'The 1989 Share Register Survey', *Economic Trends* (London: HMSO for the Central Statistical Office), January 1991, pp. 116–21.

The monetary behaviour of the different sectors of the UK economy

Fortunately, abundant information has been published on the money supply holdings of the different sectors of the UK economy. Following the Radcliffe Committee's recommendation that more money supply statistics be compiled, the Bank of England and the Office for National Statistics (formerly the Central Statistical Office) have since 1963 collected information on the bank deposits held by various categories of UK agent. The three types of private sector agent tracked in the data are the personal (or 'household') sector, the corporate sector (known more technically as 'industrial and commercial companies' or 'non-financial companies') and the financial sector (also called 'non-bank [or other] financial institutions'). Separately National Statistics has collected and published data on the asset holdings of the main types of financial institution in the UK, including their short-term assets, such as bank deposits, also from 1963. Together the sectoral money supply numbers and the information on institutions' portfolios represent a rich body of statistical material relevant to the process of asset price determination in the UK.

Sterling money balances can be held by either the public or private sectors, and by either UK resident agents or non-residents. In practice little money was held by the UK's public sector for most of the 40 years from 1963. It follows that sterling money balances had to be in the hands of UK private sector agents or in those of non-residents (mainly foreigners). If foreigners did not want to keep their money in sterling form (at the prevailing exchange rate and interest rates), they would try to offload their excess money on to UK private sector agents. As it happens, the relationship between domestic monetary policy and the exchange rate was a live and important topic for much of the 40-year period, which saw numerous currency crises. The central concern of this study, however, is the analysis of the macroeconomic consequences of excess or deficient money in the UK private sector. The households, companies and financial institutions comprising the UK private sector were, in fact, the exclusive holders of the 'money' which was officially recognised and measured in 'the monetary aggregates'.

A few words need to be said here about these aggregates. According to standard textbooks, money consists of assets with a fixed nominal value which can be used in payment to settle debts. In primitive economies precious metals were often the dominant type of money, but today hardly any currencies have an explicit metallic base. Instead notes and coin have value because they are 'legal tender' (i.e. their nominal value is enforced by law). One aggregate – M0 – consists of notes and coin ('cash'), plus banks' cash reserves which are readily converted into notes. The larger part of the money supply, however, is represented by bank deposits. A deposit is money, because a depositor can give an instruction to his bank to transfer cash to a creditor and settlement in this form is just as good as the use of cash. In fact, to pay by means of such instructions is often more convenient than to pay by cash. In the UK at the start of the 21st century the quantity of bank deposits was almost twenty times that of notes and coin. Deposits can themselves be categorised, with a common breakdown being between sight and time deposits. (Sight deposits are those that can be drawn without a notice period; time deposits can – in principle – only be drawn after a customer has given the banks some notice.) In the 1970s data were estimated for an aggregate (known as M1) which included notes, coin and sight deposits. But nowadays such data are no longer officially prepared and most attention is instead given to a so-called 'broad money measure' (M4), which includes notes, coin and all bank deposits, including time deposits. Unless otherwise specified, references to 'the quantity of money' or 'the money supply' in a UK context are to be understood as references to the M4 aggregate.

It follows – to resume the thread of the earlier discussion – that the households, companies and financial institutions comprising the UK private sector were the exclusive holders of the M4 quantity of money. It follows, further, that, for any given quantity of money, the more that was held by one sector, the less had to be held by the other two sectors. If the growth of aggregate M4 was low and one sector acquired all the extra money, the money holdings of the other two sectors could not change; if, on the other hand, the growth of aggregate M4 was extremely high and one sector did not increase its holdings at all, the money holdings of the other two sectors had to expand rapidly. All economic agents try at all times to keep their money holdings in equilibrium with their incomes and wealth – they may not succeed at every single moment, but they try – and they keep on changing their expenditure and portfolios until equilibrium is attained. The advantage of analysing the three sectors' monetary behaviour is that it produces insights into these processes of adjustment.

Table 2 on page 36 demonstrates, in a particularly striking way, clear and important differences between the sectors in the 40-year period. The growth rate of financial sector money was almost double that of the personal and corporate sectors. This reflected both the long-run institutionalisation of saving already mentioned and radical financial liberalisation. Particularly from the early 1970s, the effect of liberalisation was to enhance the competitiveness of non-bank financial institutions relative to banks and other types of business organisation. They were able profitably to expand both sides of their balance sheets, and hence their monetary assets, much faster than the quantity of money as a whole. The growth rate of financial sector money was also characterised by more pronounced volatility than that of other sectors' money. The standard deviation of the growth rates of financial sector money was four times that of personal sector money and markedly higher than that of corporate sector money.

The contrast between the different sectors' monetary behaviour is vital in understanding the transmission mechanism from money to the economy. Econometric work on the personal sector's demand-for-money functions in the UK during this period routinely found it to be stable, in the sense that standard tests on the significance of the relationship between personal sector money and a small number of other variables (including nominal incomes) were successful.[2] Similar work on the demand to hold money balances by companies and financial institutions generally failed.[3] It would be a serious mistake, however, to believe that companies' and financial institutions' monetary behaviour was so erratic as to be entirely unpredictable.

In fact, the ratio of short-term or 'liquid' assets to total assets of life assurance companies and pension funds combined was

2   Ryland Thomas, 'The demand for M4: a sectoral analysis, part I – the personal sector' (London: Bank of England, Working Paper Series no. 61, 1997); K. Alec Chrystal and L. Drake, 'Personal sector money demand in the UK', *Oxford Economic Papers* (Oxford: Clarendon Press, 1997).

3   Ryland Thomas, 'The demand for M4: a sectoral analysis, part II – the company sector' (London: Bank of England, Working Paper Series no. 62, 1997); K. Alec Chrystal, 'Company sector money demand: new evidence on the existence of a stable long-run relationship for the UK', *Journal of Money, Credit and Banking* (1994), vol. 26, pp. 479–94.

Table 2 **Key facts about different sectors' money holdings in the UK economy, 1964–2003**

	Mean increase, %	Standard deviation of growth rates
Personal sector	10.9	4.1
Corporate sector (or 'ICCs')	11.0	10.6
Financial sector (or 'OFIs')	18.3	15.7

Note: Table relates to annual changes, quarterly data, with the first rate of change calculated in Q2 1964 (note that the differences in the 'level' series are often very different from the 'changes' series published by National Statistics, because of changes in population and definition)

Source: National Statistics database, updated to 22 February 2004

much the same at the start of the 21st century as it had been in the mid-1970s, even though their assets had climbed more than 50 times[4] (see Figure 1).

Life assurance companies and pension funds were the two principal types of long-term savings institution in the UK in this period. Assets are 'liquid' if they can be quickly and cheaply converted into other assets. Bank deposits are an example of a liquid asset, but the institutions might, from time to time, also hold liquidity in assets such as short-dated Treasury or commercial bills which are not money. Indeed, the long-run stability of the ratios of money and liquidity to the total assets held by the UK institutions in the final three decades of the twentieth century was remarkable, given the wider economic turmoil and institutional upheaval of those years. It is reasonable to propose that the stability of the institutions' desired ratio of money to assets may serve the same purpose in a discussion of asset markets as Fisher's

4   See the author's 'Money and asset prices in the UK's boom–bust cycles', research papers in the May 2000 and June 2000 issues of Lombard Street Research's *Monthly Economic Review*. (The papers are available from the author at tim. congdon@lombardstreetresearch.com.)

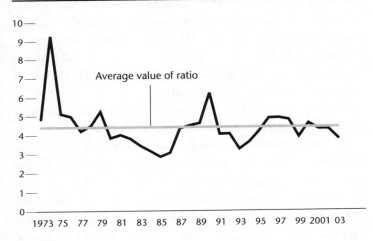

Figure 1   **The institutional 'liquidity ratio' in the UK, 1973–2003**
Ratio of liquid assets to total assets for life assurance companies and pension funds combined, %

Sources: *Financial Statistics* (London: Office for National Statistics), various issues, and author's calculations
Note: Figure shows ratio of liquid assets to total assets at life assurance companies and pension funds combined

stability of persons' desired ratio of money to expenditure in a discussion of goods markets.

The monetary behaviour of the financial institutions and asset prices: an analytical sketch

Given the long-run stability of the money/asset ratios in the UK's leading financial institutions, it is easy to sketch – in a simplified way – a link between financial sector money and asset prices. As already noted, a crucial feature of Fisher's and Friedman's descriptions of the transmission mechanism was that payments were being made within a closed circuit. As a result, if agents had excess money, individuals' attempts to unload their excess balances by increased expenditure would not change the quantity of money. Spending and national income adjusted to the quantity of money, not the quantity of money to spending and national income. An analogous argument is readily presented in the case of financial institutions in asset markets.

To help in understanding the processes at work, a highly stylised 'asset market' may be assumed. It could be regarded as a naive characterisation of Keynes's 'financial circulation'. Suppose that the UK's financial institutions are the only holders of and traders in UK equities (i.e. they operate within a closed circuit), that equities constitute all of their assets and that the stock of equities (i.e. the number of shares in issue) never changes. Suppose that – for whatever reason – the financial institutions' money balances jump sharply and that they have excess money. Whereas in the long run they try to keep their ratio of money to total assets at, say, 4 per cent, their money/assets ratio (or 'cash ratio') now stands at 6 per cent. In terms of figures, they might have £60 billion of money and £1,000 billion of equities, whereas recently they had £40 billion of money and £1,000 billion of equities. Each individual institution tries to get rid of its excess money by buying equities. *But the purchase of equities by one institution is the sale by another. For all the institutions taken together, the assumptions ensure that the flow of purchases and sales cannot change the £60 billion of money in the system.* No matter how frenetic the trading activity and no matter the keenness of particular fund managers to run down their cash, the aggregate £60 billion cannot rise or fall. The value of trading in equities in a year may be an enormous multiple of this £60 billion, but still the £60 billion cannot change.

How, then, is the 4 per cent cash ratio restored? In one round of transactions the excess supply of money causes buyers to be more eager than the sellers and the price of equities edges up, perhaps by 10 per cent, so that the value of the stock of equities is £1,100 billion. The cash ratio falls to (£60 billion divided by £1,100 billion), or just under 5.5 per cent. This is a movement towards the equilibrium 4 per cent ratio, but it is not enough. The institutions still hold 'too much money'. In the next round of transactions the excess supply of money again causes buyers to be more eager than sellers and the price of equities moves upwards again, perhaps by 15 per cent. The value of equities rises to £1,265 billion and the cash ratio drops to about 4.75 per cent. And so on. In every round the value of the money balances stays at £60 billion. *It does not change because – within the closed circuit assumed in the exercise – it cannot change.* The return of the institutions' cash ratio to the equilibrium 4 per cent is achieved, after so many rounds of transactions, by a rise in the value of equities to £1,500 billion. The institutions' asset values have adjusted to the amount of money they hold. It is a striking, but entirely realistic, feature of the example discussed that a rise in their money balances from £40 billion to £60 billion (i.e. of only £20 billion) is associated with (or 'causes') a rise in equity prices of £500 billion. The argument can be generalised freely. In the advanced economies of today, specialised financial institutions are the characteristic holders of assets. It follows that, when they hold excess money, there is likely to be upward pressure on asset prices; conversely, when they have deficient money balances, asset prices tend to fall.

Asset prices and economic activity

The realism of the analytical sketch above is very much open to question, but its value for heuristic purposes will become clear as the discussion evolves. By contrast, the claim that asset prices are relevant to spending behaviour should not need an elaborate defence. It should be sufficient to emphasise the ubiquity of arbitrage in asset markets and to note two kinds of linkage between asset markets and the rest of the economy. These linkages ensure that asset prices affect spending.

Arbitrage is important, because it links the price of equities with the price of the tangible assets and goodwill to which they relate and, at a further remove, to the price of all financial securities and all tangible assets. An excess supply of money may in the first instance boost the price of existing equities traded on the stock exchange. But that induces new issuance by listed companies and the formation of new companies with a view to seeking a quotation. Commercial real estate illustrates the processes at work. In an asset price boom, real-estate companies may be traded on the stock exchange at a premium to the value of the buildings they own, where value is assessed by chartered surveyors calculating the discounted present value of future rents. Owners of commercial property therefore package their buildings in a corporate vehicle and try to sell these vehicles to financial institutions. The market price of all property is boosted by the ambitious stock market valuations. In a modern economy similar processes are at work for all assets. Further, arbitrage operates between different assets as well as between different forms of the same asset. If equities rise sharply in price, they may appear overvalued relative to commercial or residential property. The wide variety of wealth-holders found in a modern economy – including rich individuals and companies, as well as the large financial institutions – may then sell equities and use the proceeds to buy property. The excess supply of money – the condition of 'too much money chasing too few assets' – has pervasive effects.

Of course, the power of arbitrage to remove asset price anomalies relies on the ability to switch payments between different types of asset market. A key assumption in the analysis – that of a specialised asset market, which constitutes a closed circuit where certain asset prices are set – has to be relaxed. Instead agents compare prices in all asset markets, and sell overvalued assets in one market and buy undervalued assets in another. (Not only do they sell overvalued stocks to buy undervalued stocks and sell small-capitalisation stocks to buy big-capitalisation stocks and so on, but they also sell houses to buy shares and sell shares to buy houses.) Does that destroy the concept of a closed circuit of payments in which the ability of excess or deficient money to alter asset prices depends on the quantity of money being a given? The short answer, in an economy without international transactions, is 'not at all'.[5]

It is true, for example, that – if quoted equities become expensive relative to unquoted companies of the same type – the owners of unquoted companies will float them, which withdraws money from the pool of institutional funds. Conversely, when quoted companies become cheap relative to 'asset value',

---

5   Of course, every economy has international transactions. Such transactions represent another escape valve for an excess supply or demand for money balances, in accordance with the monetary approach to the balance of payments. But to discuss the possibilities would take the paper too far. In any case, the incorporation of 'an overseas sector' in data-sets on transactions in particular assets is conceptually straightforward (see Table 3 in the main text). The overseas sector's transactions become entries in the capital account of the balance of payments.

Table 3 Asset markets in the UK in 1994

1 The market in quoted ordinary shares (equities)

Net sellers of equities	Amount sold, £m	Net buyers of equities	Amount bought, £m
Banks	393	Life assurance and	
Personal sector	679	pension funds	8,531
Industrial and		Remaining financial	
commercial companies	9,261	institutions	1,097
Public sector	3,646	Overseas sector	4,351
Sum of sales		Sum of purchases	
by net sellers	13,979	by net buyers	13,979

Note: Each of the identified types of equity market participant had substantial purchases *and* sales. The gross value of their transactions was a very high multiple of their net purchases and sales. Stock exchange turnover in UK and Irish listed equities was £577,526 million in 1994. (In 1994 the UK's gross domestic product at market prices was about £670,000 million.)

Source: *Financial Statistics* (London: Office for National Statistics), June 1998 issue, Tables 8.2A and 6.3A

2 The market in unquoted ordinary shares

Net sellers of unquoted ordinary shares	Amount sold, £m	Net buyers of unquoted ordinary shares	Amount bought, £m
Remaining financial	3,430	Banks and	1,929
institutions		building societies	
Public sector	726	Life assurance and	
Personal sector	1,890	pension funds	106
		Industrial and	
		commercial companies	694
		Overseas sector	3,317
Sum of sales		Sum of purchases	
by net sellers	6,046	by net buyers	6,046

Note: Again, each of the different types of market participant would have had substantial purchases *and* sales, although gross turnover would have been much smaller than with quoted equities. Transactions would have included successful business people selling out to corporate entities.

Source: *Financial Statistics*, June 1998, Table 8.2B

3 *The market in UK company bonds and preference shares*

Net sellers of bonds and prefs	Amount sold, £m	Net buyers of bonds and prefs	Amount bought, £m
Remaining financial institutions	10,378	Banks and building societies	2,312
Industrial and commercial companies	7,215	Overseas sector	16,039
Central government	2,276	Life assurance and pension funds	1,449
		Personal sector	69
Sum of sales by net sellers	19,869	Sum of purchases by net buyers	19,869

The sum of net sales and purchases was zero.

Note: Again, each of the different types of market participant would have had substantial purchases and sales.

Source: *Financial Statistics*, June 1998, Table 8.2C

entrepreneurs organise takeovers, which inject money back into the institutional pool. To the extent that one type of participant has been a net buyer and it has satisfied its purchases by drawing on its bank balances, its bank deposits (i.e. its money holdings) must fall. But the money balances of another type of agent must rise. In fact, it is possible to identify particular types of participant in asset markets, and to collect data on their purchases and sales. Table 3 gives data on the markets in UK quoted ordinary shares, UK unquoted ordinary shares, and UK bonds and preference shares in 1994.[6] These markets might be thought of as belonging, archetypically, to Keynes's 'financial circulation'. The net value of purchases and sales in a particular market, and indeed of all asset purchases and sales in the economy as a whole, is zero. But the

---

6 The reader may ask, 'Why 1994?' The answer is that the data in Table 3 are no longer prepared – or, at any rate, they are no longer published – by the UK's official statistical agency.

logically necessary equivalence of the value of purchases and sales does not mean that the prices of the assets bought and sold cannot change. In particular, prices change when all the agents participating in the numerous asset markets have excess or deficient money holdings. The arena of payments – the closed circuit within which the transactions take place – becomes the entire economy.[7]

What about the two kinds of influence of asset prices on spending on goods and services? First, investment in new capital items occurs when the market value of assets is above their replacement cost. If the value of an office building was £10 million and it cost only £5 million to purchase the land and build it, it would obviously be profitable for an entrepreneur to organise the construction of the new office building. On the other hand, if

7   It is conceptually straightforward – although empirically very demanding – to expand the arena of payments, the closed circuit for transactions, so that it becomes the world economy. For small- and medium-sized economies the effect of differences in money growth rates on the exchange rate is an important element in the transmission mechanism from money to economic activity and the price level. In the UK policy debate in the 1970s and 1980s the relationship between money and the exchange rate was much noticed, and some economists even thought that the exchange rate was the key asset price influenced by money supply trends. The work of David Laidler and Michael Parkin at the Manchester Inflation Workshop was influential in spreading so-called 'international monetarism'. (See, for example, the papers in Michael Parkin and George Zis [eds], *Inflation in Open Economies* [Manchester: University of Manchester Press, 1976].) The ideas were developed at the London Business School, with well-known papers from James Ball, Alan Budd and Terence Burns. (See, again, for example, James Ball and Terence Burns, 'The inflationary mechanism in the UK economy', *American Economic Review* [Nashville, TN: American Economic Association, 1976], vol. 66, pp. 467–84.) One purpose of this study is to show that excess money growth in the UK affects not only the equilibrium sterling price of *foreign* assets (and foreign-produced goods and services), but also the equilibrium sterling price of *domestic* assets. The view that exchange rate adjustment was the heart of the transmission mechanism was given too much prominence in the UK policy debate in the 1970s and 1980s. Exchange rate adjustment is a significant part of the transmission mechanism, but only a part.

the value of a building was lower than the replacement cost, no investment would take place. Assets will continue to be bought and sold, and investments will be undertaken or suspended, until the market value of assets is brought into equivalence with their replacement value.[8] Second, consumption is affected by changing levels of wealth. When asset price gains increase people's wealth, they are inclined to spend more out of income.[9]

Another way of stating the wider theme is to emphasise that, in the real world, markets in goods and services and markets in assets interact constantly. Keynes's two circulations – the 'industrial circulation' and the 'financial circulation' – are not separate.[10]

---

8   The idea that investment adjusts until the market value of a capital asset equals the replacement cost is associated with James Tobin and 'the Q ratio', i.e. the ratio of market value of a firm's capital to its replacement cost. See his article, 'A general equilibrium approach to monetary theory', *Journal of Money, Credit and Banking* (1969), vol. 1, pp. 15–29. But similar remarks have been made by many economists, including Friedman. See his 'The lag in effect of monetary policy', in Friedman, *The Optimum Quantity of Money* (London and Basingstoke: Macmillan, 1969), pp. 237–60, reprinted from a paper in 1961 in *The Journal of Political Economy*, and, in particular, pp. 255–6. When an excess supply of money affects asset markets, the result is 'to raise the prices of houses relative to the rents of dwelling units, or the cost of purchasing a car relative to the cost of renting one', and so on. In Friedman's view, 'the process operates through the balance sheet, and it is plausible that balance-sheet adjustments are sluggish in the sense that individuals spread adjustments over a considerable period of time' (p. 256).

9   Numerous studies identify a relationship between wealth and consumption. See, for example, J. Byrne and E. P. Davis, 'Disaggregate wealth and aggregate consumption: an investigation of empirical relationships in the G7', *National Institute of Economic and Social Research Discussion Paper*, no. 180 (London: National Institute, 2001).

10 Keynes dropped the notions of separate industrial and financial 'circulations' in *The General Theory*, preferring instead to analyse the demand for money in terms of different motives for a particular holder rather than in terms of different holders. 'Money held for each of three purposes forms, nevertheless, a single pool, which the holder is under no necessity to segregate into … water-tight compartments.' (Keynes, *The General Theory of Employment, Interest and Money* [London: Macmillan & Co., Papermac reprint 1964, originally published 1936], p. 195.)

If excess money in the financial sector causes asset price gains, agents of all kinds will be inclined to sell a portion of their assets and buy more goods and services (i.e. to spend a higher proportion of their incomes). On the other hand, if deficient money in the financial sector causes asset price falls, agents will spend a lower proportion of their incomes on goods and services. The adequacy of money balances relative to a desired level, the direction of pressures on asset prices and wealth-influenced changes in the propensity to spend out of income should be seen as an indissoluble whole.[11]

Before reviewing the realism of our account of money's role in asset markets, a polemical note can be injected into the discussion. In none of the above has a reference been made to 'interest rates'. Agents have been adjusting their spending on goods and

---

11 An implication is that the circular flow of income and expenditure – such a familiar part of undergraduate macroeconomic courses – is misleading and unrealistic when it is taken to imply that national income stays in line with national expenditure unless autonomous injections of demand come from the government or overseas. Any agent can sell any asset, obtain a money balance and use the proceeds to buy a good or service that constitutes part of national output, and the purchase leads to increased national income and expenditure. Similarly, any agent can run down a money balance and buy a good or service, with the same effects. Assets differ from money in that the nominal value of money is given, whereas the nominal value of assets can vary without limit. The transactions involved in 'mortgage equity withdrawal' from the housing market – at present a topic of much interest – illustrate the merging of asset markets and markets in current goods and services. Much research on this topic has been conducted at the Bank of England. See, for example, M. Davey, 'Mortgage equity withdrawal and consumption', *Bank of England Quarterly Bulletin* (London: Bank of England, 2001), spring 2001 issue, pp. 100–103. The author introduced the concept of mortgage equity withdrawal to the analysis of personal sector spending in a paper written jointly with Paul Turnbull in 1982. (Tim Congdon and Paul Turnbull, 'The coming boom in housing credit', L. Messel & Co. research paper, June 1982, reprinted in Tim Congdon, *Reflections on Monetarism* [Aldershot: Edward Elgar for the Institute of Economic Affairs, 1992], pp. 274–87.)

services, and their asset portfolios, in response to excess or deficient money, and the prices of goods, services and assets have been changing in order to bring agents back into 'monetary equilibrium' (i.e. a condition where the demand to hold money balances equals the supply of such balances). The Bank of England's version of the transmission mechanism in its 1999 note to the Treasury Committee – like the innumerable other accounts in which interest rates do all the work – is far from being the only way of approaching the subject or a definitive statement of the matter.

What about 'the rate of interest'?

A further point needs to be recognised. The lack of an explicit reference to 'interest rates' does not mean they are absent from the discussion. Indeed, they are present implicitly whenever the price of an asset is mentioned. If the expected income stream from an asset is given, its yield varies inversely with the price. If the yield – denoting the income return – is taken to be a similar expression to 'the rate of interest', the determination of the level of an asset price becomes equivalent to the determination of 'the rate of interest'. This is most clear if the discussion is confined – as in some accounts of Keynes's *General Theory* – to an economy with non-interest-bearing money and fixed-interest bonds. In equilibrium the expected return from holding the bond just compensates the saver for the loss of the convenience associated with holding money. It follows that, if an existing equilibrium is disturbed by an increase in the quantity of money, the equilibrium bond price ought to rise and 'the rate of interest' to fall. *The General Theory*, macroeconomics textbooks and academic journals devote a huge amount of attention to a particular case where this normal reaction is not found; they identify a possible perverse outcome – the celebrated 'liquidity trap' – in which 'the rate of interest' does not fall any further when the quantity of money increases. (The explanation is that investors fear a future capital loss from holding bonds at high prices and so are not prepared to drive them up further.) In a liquidity trap monetary policy appears to be ineffective. In *The General Theory* Keynes magnified the trap's importance, arguing that it might become a fatal flaw of market capitalism and a powerful justification for 'a somewhat comprehensive socialisation of investment'.[12] He did concede, however, that – when he was writing in the mid-1930s – he knew of no example of a liquidity trap in the real world. Professor Paul Krugman of Princeton University has claimed more recently that Japan suffered from a liquidity trap in the late 1990s, because its economy failed to achieve a convincing recovery when the Bank of Japan reduced its discount rate to zero.[13]

But Keynes's presentation of the liquidity trap in *The General Theory* was a special argument about an economy with only two assets (i.e. money and bonds). A more realistic economy is replete with a highly diverse range of assets, many of which have quite different price dynamics from fixed-interest bonds. Nowadays equities and real estate, both residential and commercial, are more important in most portfolios than bonds. It remains true that

---

12 In a footnote to p. 309 of *The General Theory* Keynes quoted from Bagehot, 'John Bull can stand many things, but he cannot stand 2 per cent.' In the final chapter he claimed that, since 'it seems unlikely that the influence of banking policy on the rate of interest will be sufficient by itself to determine an optimum rate of investment', the state should undertake 'a somewhat comprehensive socialisation of investment' (Keynes, *The General Theory*, p. 378).

13 Paul Krugman, *The Return of Depression Economics* (London: Allen Lane for the Penguin Press, 1999), pp. 70–77.

wealth-holders have to balance at the margin the relative attractions of money and these assets. As argued in earlier sections, the effect of an increase in the quantity of money is to cause several rounds of portfolio rebalancing, and to raise the equilibrium price of equities and real estate.[14] With the dividend stream given, an increase in the price of equities is equivalent to a reduction in the dividend yield that they pay (or 'the rate of interest' on equities, if the reader prefers to put it like that); with the rental stream given, an increase in the price of real estate is equivalent to a reduction in the rental yield ('the rate of interest') on real estate; and so on. We can make similar statements about 'the rate of interest' on almost any asset we care to consider. To confine the discussion to 'bonds', and to 'the rate of interest' on bonds, is a gross misrepresentation. Many textbooks, influenced by *The General Theory*, suffer from this habit. They should have been rewritten decades ago.[15]

---

14 Note that this is only a *partial and temporary* equilibrium. After a jump in the quantity of money a rise in the price of equities may restore equilibrium between the quantity of money and the value of the equity market and real estate, but it may disturb a pre-existing equilibrium between, on the one hand, the market value of equities and real estate, and, on the other, the replacement cost of capital assets. Further decisions, and more rounds of adjustment, are then motivated, as agents try to restore equilibrium between the market value of assets and their replacement cost. Of course, in a *general and complete* equilibrium all the equilibrium conditions must be satisfied.

15 A standard text – *Macroeconomics* by Dornbusch and Fischer – says, in a discussion of the demand for money, 'The wealth budget constraint in the assets markets states that the demand for real balances ... plus the demand for real bond holdings ... must add up to the real financial wealth of the individual.' So, 'the decision to hold real money balances is also a decision to hold less real wealth in the form of bonds' (Rudiger Dornbusch and Stanley Fischer, *Macroeconomics* [New York: McGraw-Hill, 6th edn, 1994], p. 103). Surprisingly, this restriction of wealth to the sum of money and bonds follows shortly after an account of real-world assets, which refers at some length to equities and housing. Keynes himself – although not apparently succeeding generations of textbook writers – understood the dangerously specific way in which he talked of 'the rate of interest' in

Further, the shift of focus towards equities as the dominant alternative asset to money generates an argument that makes the liquidity trap highly implausible. In our analytical sketch of the monetary determination of asset prices, it was clear that increases in financial sector money raised the equilibrium level of equity prices. The impact on investment depended largely on the relationship between the market price of equities and the replacement cost of buildings, plant and equipment. In a world where the only two assets are money and equities, injections of extra money boost the market price of equities and reduce their equilibrium dividend yield. It is possible – as in an economy with only money and bonds – that the dividend yield falls to an unusually low level and that additional money injections cannot persuade investors to drive the dividend yield down further. Monetary policy would seem to be as ineffective as in a bond-dominated economy.

But would that make sense? Notice what is being said here. It is being claimed that monetary policy cannot work because – although the dividend yield is low and equity prices are high – extra money will not push equity prices to even more ambitious levels. Another equilibrium condition has to be remembered, the need for the market price of equities to be equal to the replacement cost of buildings, plant and equipment. In almost any conceivable real-world situation, a low dividend yield on equities ('a bull

The General Theory. In a footnote on p. 151 he remarked, 'In my *Treatise on Money* … I pointed out that when a company's shares are quoted very high so that it can raise capital by issuing more shares on favourable terms, this has the same effect as if it could borrow at a low rate of interest' (the quotation is from the 1964 Macmillan Papermac edition of *The General Theory*). Whether one talks in terms of interest rates and asset yields, or in terms of the market value of assets in comparison with their economic value and replacement cost, is to some extent a matter of taste.

market', in more familiar parlance) implies that their market price is above replacement cost. This encourages people to order new capital goods and sell them for a profit, and buoyant economic activity is indeed the characteristic accompaniment of equity bull markets. Keynes was wise to concede in *The General Theory* that he knew of no real-world example of a liquidity trap. Its plausibility depended on the rarefied assumption of an economy where the only two assets were money and bonds. A more realistic and sensible framework for the analysis of the relationship between money and asset prices is long overdue.[16]

The realism of the analytical sketch: what is the direction of causation?

A central motif of the argument has been that spending and asset prices change in response to the quantity of money, not that the quantity of money responds to spending and asset prices. Many economists, however, dispute this view of the direction of causation. In an early critique of Friedman's work, Kaldor claimed that the quantity of money was determined by national income rather than national income by the quantity of money.[17]

16　A good example of the contemporary neglect of the role of money in asset price determination is Schiller's well-regarded *Irrational Exuberance*. The book analyses the stock market excesses of the late 1990s without a single reference to a monetary aggregate. A few pages are devoted to the possible role of monetary policy in preventing bubbles, but monetary policy is reduced to 'interest rate policies' (see p. 225 of Robert J. Schiller, *Irrational Exuberance* [Princeton, NJ: Princeton University Press, 2000]).

17　Nicholas Kaldor, 'The new monetarism', *Lloyds Bank Review* (London: Lloyds Bank), July 1970 issue, pp. 1–17, reprinted on pp. 261–78 of Alan Walters (ed.), *Money and Banking: Selected Readings* (Harmondsworth: Penguin Education, 1973). See, in particular, p. 268 in the book of papers edited by Walters.

In discussing Friedman's demonstration of the historical stability of money's velocity of circulation, Kaldor said that stable velocity had been maintained 'only because ... the supply of money was unstable'. The explanation was that 'in one way or another, an increased demand for money evoked an increase in supply'. The amount of money 'accommodated' to 'the needs of trade', possibly because the official objective of 'financial stabilisation' kept interest rates constant at a particular level or possibly because the central bank and the government wished to ensure 'an orderly market for government debt'. Kaldor's remarks begged several new questions, as the description of money supply creation was rather unclear. A fair summary, however, is that he thought that – if agents had an excess supply of or demand for money – banks' customers would talk to their bank managers, and take the necessary action to reduce or increase the size of their money balances and so restore it to the desired, equilibrium figure. If the customers had excess money, they would reduce their bank borrowings and contract the quantity of money; if their money balances were deficient, they would increase their bank borrowings and so create more money. The quantity of money would therefore be 'endogenous'; it would react to 'the needs of trade' (i.e. national income), not the other way round.

Similar statements have also been made about the relationship between financial sector money and asset prices. It is said that if agents' money holdings are out of kilter with the rest of their portfolios they can easily change the quantity of money without any effect on asset prices or other macroeconomic variables. Some of the most forthright such statements have come from Minford. One example appeared in a 1996 paper from the Liverpool Research Group. In Minford's words,

> How much is held on deposit depends on investors; and
> whether they hold these deposits in banks, building societies
> or other close competitors will depend on their relative
> terms – interest rates and service. However much you
> change the definition of money it will be a volatile quantity,
> as depositors switch from markets to cash and between
> institutions inside and outside the definitions.[18]

In short, according to this thesis, if agents have excess money, they *as individuals* try to get rid of the surplus balances by switching to a close alternative asset, and the consequence of all these attempts is to reduce the quantity of money *in the aggregate* and thereby eliminate the excess money. Indeed, Minford has made statements about asset portfolios that imply they can be restructured or reorganised to any extent, and yet still make no difference to macroeconomic outcomes. In his words, 'There is literally an infinite number of asset-liability combinations in which the private sector can hold its savings; and each is as good as the other from its viewpoint.' In his book on *The Supply Side Revolution in Britain* he exemplified the argument by a reference to unit trusts. In his words, the formation of a new unit trust may have the result that

> … there are more private sector assets and liabilities; but
> savings are the same and so are interest rates. As a result
> nothing has changed to make people want to spend more
> or do anything differently. All that has happened is a
> reshuffling of balance sheets.[19]

---

18   Patrick Minford, paper from Liverpool Research Group, summer 1996. The passage was discussed in Tim Congdon, 'An open letter to Professor Patrick Minford', *Monthly Economic Review* (London: Gerrard & National, July 1996), pp. 3–12.

19   Patrick Minford, *The Supply Side Revolution in Britain* (Aldershot: Edward Elgar for the Institute of Economic Affairs), p. 70.

By extension, if banks add to their balance sheets by making new loans or purchasing securities, the resulting increase in their deposit liabilities (i.e. in the quantity of money) does not cause people to want 'to spend more or do anything differently'. The extra assets and liabilities cancel out, and net wealth is unchanged. According to Minford, the increase in bank deposits therefore has no relevance to other macroeconomic variables.

To summarise, the Minford argument has two parts. The first part says that, as financial institutions' assets and liabilities must be equal, their net wealth is always nil and cannot at any time be relevant to expenditure. The second asserts the infinite plasticity of balance sheets, that any transaction – 'reshuffling' to use his term – may alter the composition of the balance sheet, but changes in composition are irrelevant to the wider economy. Any consequences are contained within the financial system, and so have no bearing on 'savings' and 'the interest rate', which – in the Minford scheme – evidently do matter.

The Minford argument is discussed in some detail in this study, because it has had considerable influence on UK policy-making. Minford has used it to challenge the macroeconomic significance of broadly defined money measures, and he is the leading exponent in the UK of the view that narrowly defined money measures (such as M0) are crucial to the economy's behaviour. Sir Alan Walters, who was economic adviser to Mrs Thatcher when she was prime minister in the 1980s, also belongs to what might be termed 'the narrow money school'. In his *Britain's Economic Renaissance* he proposed a definition of money in which the use of money in retail transactions was highlighted. But his preference is for a somewhat wider measure (i.e. M1, including what he terms 'checkable accounts') than Minford.[20]

A factual and statistical account of historical episodes characterised by large asset price movements may throw light on the validity of the arguments from Kaldor and the narrow-money school, and help to settle the debate about the direction of causation. That is the work of the next two chapters.

---

20 Alan Walters, *Britain's Economic Renaissance* (Oxford: Oxford University Press, 1986), pp. 116–17.

3 MONEY AND ASSET PRICES IN THE UK'S BOOM–BUST CYCLES

The causal role of money growth fluctuations in asset price volatility may be better appreciated by recalling the experience of two particularly big cycles in the UK, that between late 1971 and 1974 ('the Heath–Barber boom' and the stock market and property crashes of 1974) and that between 1985 and 1992 ('the Lawson boom' and the ensuing recession), and by reviewing the events of a more recent and fortunately much milder cyclical episode (the mini-boom of 1996–98). The economy's instability in the Heath–Barber and Lawson booms was notorious, and contrasts with relative stability in most of the other 40 years from 1963.

An overview of the main facts about money growth and the economy in this 40-year period may be a helpful preface to the detailed narrative. In the first 25 years after World War II, UK policy-makers had suppressed inflation by a variety of non-market methods, including direct controls on prices and wages. In the monetary sphere the favoured approach was to curb the growth of bank balance sheets, usually by a crude quantitative limit on bank advances. But in September 1971 the banking system was liberalised in a set of reforms known as 'Competition and Credit Control'. The banks were to be free to expand their businesses as they wished, while 'the authorities' (i.e. the government and the Bank of England) would raise interest rates to prevent exces-

Figure 2   **Money and national income, 1964–2003**
*Annual % changes in M4 and GDP at current market prices,
quarterly data seasonally adjusted, %*

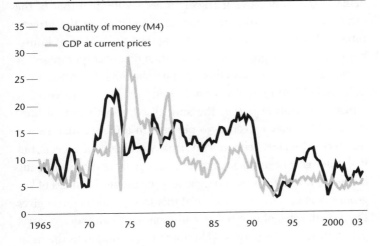

Source: Office for National Statistics website

sive money supply expansion. In practice officialdom was often reluctant to administer the interest rate medicine and credit booms continued for far too long. The September 1971 reforms were followed by over twenty years of macroeconomic volatility, with large fluctuations in the growth of bank credit and money, even more dramatic swings in asset prices, and somewhat smaller fluctuations in the growth of nominal national income. Figure 2 portrays the growth rates of money and nominal gross domestic product in the 40 years to 2003, with the turbulence of the middle two decades being evident in both series.

Chapter 2 noted that the different sectors of the economy

– households, companies and financial institutions – displayed different monetary behaviours. More precisely, households' demand for money was markedly more stable than that of the other two sectors, with the standard deviation of the growth rates of financial sector money being four times that of household money and significantly higher than that of corporate sector money. Figure 3 illustrates this contrast, showing the growth rates of household and non-household money during the 40 years. A remarkable feature is that the annualised growth rate of non-household money exceeded 30 per cent in no fewer than twelve quarters.[1] Monetary economics has many problematic aspects, but it should have been obvious to all policy-makers that something had gone wrong in an economy where the money balances of key groups of agents were exploding at this sort of rate. Figure 4 gives the growth rates of non-household money and an index of asset prices in the same period. (The method of compiling the asset price index is explained in an annexe to Chapter 6.) Asset prices were more volatile than either money or nominal GDP over the four decades, but the relationship between changes in non-household money and asset prices was not of markedly worse quality than that between changes in more familiar monetary variables and nominal GDP.

---

1   The twelve quarters were Q3 1967, Q3 1972, Q4 1972, Q1 1973, Q3 1973, Q4 1977, Q1 1978, Q2 1981, Q1 1986, Q3 1986, Q1 1987 and Q3 1987. With two exceptions, all these quarters coincided with extreme asset price buoyancy. (The exceptions were Q3 1967, which was affected by the devaluation of the pound, and Q2 1981.)

Figure 3 **Household and non-household money in the UK, 1963–2003**
Annualised growth rate in quarter, %

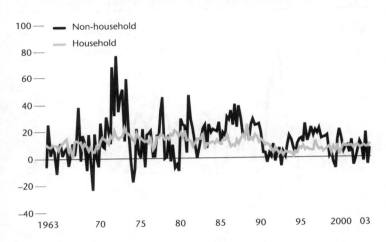

Sources: Office for National Statistics website and author's calculations

Financial sector money and asset prices in the Heath–Barber boom

The first of the boom–bust cycles is usually named after Edward Heath, who was prime minister at the time, and Anthony Barber, who was Chancellor of the Exchequer. As already noted, the Competition and Credit Control reforms of September 1971 were intended to end quantitative restrictions on bank credit, which had been in force for most of the preceding 30 years. Rapid growth in bank credit and, hence, in a broadly defined measure of money followed in 1972 and 1973. In the year to the third quarter 1970 M4 increased by 10.7 per cent and in the year to Q3 1971 it increased

Figure 4   **Non-household money and asset prices, 1964–2004**
*Annual changes in M4 held by companies and financial institutions
(i.e., non-households) and an asset price index, quarterly data, %*

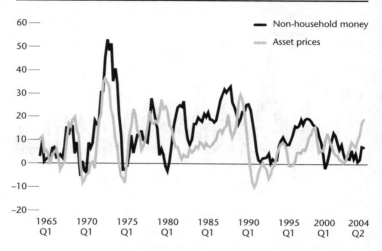

Sources: Office for National Statistics website and author's calculations for non-household money
and see appendix

by 14.1 per cent. In the following two years M4 advanced by 22.0 per cent and 23.0 per cent respectively.[2] The difference in the monetary behaviours of the economy's sectors was particularly clear in the cycle of the early 1970s. In the year to Q3 1970 personal sector money increased by 11.5 per cent and in the year to Q3 1972 by 13.7 per cent, both figures being roughly in line with total

2   *Economic Trends: Annual Supplement* (London: National Statistics, 2002 edn), p. 245. The data on changes in the sectors' money balances in the following paragraphs come from the database in the National Statistics website, as it was in the spring of 2004.

M4 growth. But in the next two years the underlying stability of personal sector money meant that it did not increase by as much as total M4, and it rose by 16.3 per cent and 18.5 per cent respectively.

Recalling the discussion in Chapter 2, the households, companies and financial institutions comprising the UK private sector were the only holders of M4 money. For any given quantity of money, the less that was held by one sector, the more that had to be held by the other two sectors. Logically, the shortfall in personal sector money growth in 1972 and 1973 implied an extremely sharp acceleration in the growth rates of corporate and financial sector money. In the years to Q3 1970 and Q3 1971 corporate sector money grew by 2.7 per cent and 22.2 per cent respectively; in the year to Q3 1972 it soared by 48.2 per cent and in the year to Q3 1973 by 39.2 per cent. The violence of the change in corporate balance sheets between the two years before the boom and the two years of the boom itself is obvious. It was, however, overshadowed by even more extreme movements in financial sector money. In the year to Q3 1970 financial sector money increased by 22.8 per cent and in the following year it fell slightly, by 1.3 per cent. But in the year to Q3 1972 it jumped by 75.0 per cent and in the year to Q3 1973 by 46.0 per cent!

Further insights are gained by extending the analysis to particular types of institution and seeing how they responded to the money supply shock. Friedman's game of musical chairs – as agents interacted to bring money balances to a desired amount after an unexpected change to such balances – was played at the level of the thousands of organisations that belonged to the financial sector, as well as at the level of the three sectors that constituted the UK private sector. At the end of 1971 life assurance

Figure 5   **The explosion in financial institutions' liquidity in the Heath–Barber boom**
Value of short-term assets held by life offices and pension funds at end-year, £m

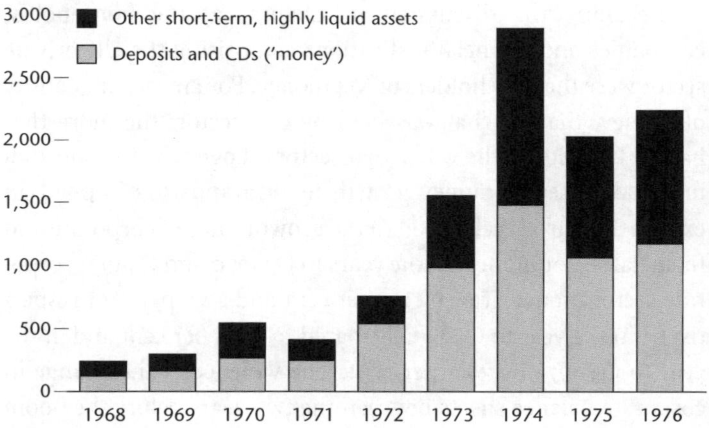

Source: *Financial Statistics* (London: Central Statistical Office), various issues

companies had short-term assets (mostly bank deposits) of £349 million. In 1972 these short-term assets leapt by £202.3 million (by 58.0 per cent) and in 1973 by a further £201.1 million (36.5 per cent). At the end of 1971 private sector pension funds had short-term assets of £144 million. In 1972 they increased by £74.0 million (51.4 per cent) and in 1973 by another £170.3 million (almost 80 per cent!).[3]

What happened to asset prices? At the time corporate bonds

---

3   *Financial Statistics* (London: Central Statistical Office), December 1974 issue, pp. 89 and 93.

and government fixed-interest securities (or 'gilts') were a large part of life company and pension fund assets, but some observers were concerned that high money supply growth would lead to inflation and higher interest rates, and that higher interest rates would decimate the value of bonds and gilts. (These observers – such as Professor Alan Day of the London School of Economics, Peter Jay of *The Times* and Gordon Pepper of W. Greenwell & Co., the stockbrokers – were correct.) The institutions therefore wanted to increase their equity weightings (i.e. the proportion of their total assets in equities) while their money balances were exploding at annual rates of between 30 and 80 per cent. As suggested in the analytical sketch above, the individual fund managers wanted to keep their cash ratios down, but if they bought securities they would be buying them mostly from other institutions. To use Minford's word, the money would be 'reshuffled' between them. But they would continue to have excess money holdings until share prices had increased. In practice stock exchange turnover soared and share prices rose dramatically. The FT Industrial Ordinary Index of shares climbed from 322.8 (1 July 1935 = 100) in May 1971 to 533.7 a year later, an increase of 65.3 per cent.[4]

Unfortunately, that was not the end of the story. The early 1970s were a period of considerable political and social uncertainty, and share prices were constrained by heavy selling by the personal sector. May 1972 was the stock market peak. Asset price buoyancy in the rest of 1972 and during 1973 was instead most marked in property. Both residential and commercial property registered enormous price increases, at a pace never before

---

4   The figures for the FT Industrial Ordinary Index are monthly averages.

recorded in the UK's peacetime history. The economy as a whole was profoundly affected. The increase in real domestic demand in 1973 was 7.8 per cent, almost the highest figure in the post-war period. The sequel to the cyclical excesses was a dramatic rise in inflation (to over 25 per cent in early 1975) and the worst recession since the 1930s, as policy-makers struggled to bring inflation down to an internationally acceptable figure.

One cause of the slide in activity was a severe squeeze on company liquidity in 1974, which was a by-product of a decline in aggregate money supply growth. In the year to the end of 1973, M4 rose by 22.1 per cent, but in the year to end-1974 it increased much more slowly, by only 10.8 per cent. The swing from monetary ease to restraint can be seen as more abrupt if one considers the inflation-adjusted rate of money growth, because inflation was higher in 1974 than in 1973. Corporate and financial sector money saw more extreme movements than aggregate money in the downturn, in line with the long-run behaviour patterns and just as they had in the upturn. In the year to Q4 1973 financial sector money advanced by 35.1 per cent; in the first three quarters of 1974 it contracted. Share prices started to fall in late 1973 and plunged in 1974, with the FT Industrial Ordinary Index in November at little more than a third of its value in May 1972. Corporate sector money climbed by over a third in the year to Q4 1973, but declined by almost a tenth in the year to Q4 1974. Companies' attempts to protect their balance sheets were responsible for heavy run-downs in stocks and cutbacks in investment, while commercial property values slumped.

Financial sector money and asset prices in the Lawson boom

After the recession of 1980 and 1981, the early 1980s were a fairly quiet period in which output grew at a rate that was slightly above trend, inflation was stable at about 5 per cent a year, employment increased gradually and asset markets were steady. But in late 1985 a drastic change in monetary policy occurred, comparable in its cyclical consequences to Competition and Credit Control in 1971. The growth of the quantity of money had been held back in the early 1980s partly by a technique known as 'over-funding'. This involved sales of government debt to non-banks in excess of the budget deficit, and led to reductions in banks' assets and their deposit liabilities. For technical reasons apparently related to money market management, over-funding was stopped in the autumn of 1985. Broad money targets were suspended and, in due course, they were to be abandoned. An acceleration of money supply growth quickly became clear. Whereas M4 growth averaged 13.0 per cent in the four years to end-1985, it averaged 16.9 per cent in the following four years.[5]

The contrast in monetary conditions before and after autumn 1985 was in fact greater than implied by this 4-per-cent-a-year difference in the annual growth rates. A big fall in oil prices cut UK inflation in 1986 and dampened inflation expectations. The increase in personal incomes remained fairly steady in 1986 and 1987, and the rise in the personal sector's money holdings was more or less constant – at a little above 11.5 per cent a year – from 1983 to 1987. The result – as in the Heath–Barber boom – was that the upturn in aggregate M4 growth led to an explosion in the

5   *Economic Trends: Annual Supplement*, 2002 edn, p. 245.

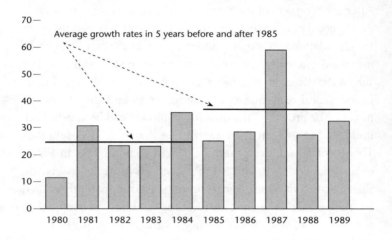

Figure 6 **Growth of financial sector money, before and after 1985**
Annual change in M4 held by non-bank financial institutions, %

Source: Office for National Statistics website

money holdings of companies and financial institutions. In the four years to 1985 companies' M4 holdings grew on average by 11.6 per cent; in 1986 and 1987 they increased by 30.3 per cent and 19.2 per cent respectively. Financial institutions were in a somewhat different position, because a sequence of liberalisation measures had encouraged their rapid growth in the early 1980s, and much of this growth is best interpreted as a benign, once-and-for-all adjustment in their economic importance. The average growth rate of financial institutions' money holdings in the five years from 1980 to 1984 inclusive was a very high 24.8 per cent. Even so, in the next five years – the years of the Lawson boom – the average growth rate was about 10 per cent a year more, at 34.4 per cent (see Figure 6).

The upturn in the growth rate of non-personal money holdings was particularly marked in 1986 and 1987. Indeed, in 1987 financial institutions' money holdings jumped by 58.9 per cent, a figure that was comparable with their experience in the Heath–Barber boom fifteen years earlier. Again it is easy to trace a relationship between the money balances held by the financial sector as a whole and those held by particular types of institution. At the end of 1985 life assurance companies had £3,262 million held in 'cash and balances with the monetary sector' and £123 million held in certificates of deposit (CD); at the end of 1986 the corresponding figures were £4,062 million and £173 million; and at the end of 1987 they were £5,975 million and £188 million.[6] At the end of 1985 pension funds had £3,970 million held in 'cash and balances with banks' and £156 million in CDs; at the end of 1986 the corresponding figures were £5,697 million and £229 million; and at the end of 1987 they were £8,263 million and £570 million.[7] So the money balances of these two types of institution together advanced from £7,511 million at the end of 1985 to £10,161 million at the end of 1986 (or by 35.3 per cent) and to £14,996 million at the end of 1987 (representing 47.6 per cent growth in 1987). In two years they almost exactly doubled, while financial sector money in aggregate increased by 104 per cent.

And what happened to asset prices in this cycle? Table 1 showed that by the late 1980s insurance companies and pension funds owned about half of all UK equities, while other types of long-term

---

6   *Financial Statistics* (London: Central Statistical Office), July 1987 and April 1989 issues, Table 7.13 in both issues.

7   Ibid., Table 7.14 in both issues.

savings institution (unit trust groups and investment trusts) held at least another 10 per cent. It is therefore unsurprising that the surge in these institutions' money holdings should be associated with large stock market gains. In the two years to September 1987 – which, roughly speaking, were the first two years from the end of over-funding and the consequent acceleration in money supply growth – the FT All Share Index rose from 633.18 to 1,174.38. In other words, share prices doubled. Share prices behaved much like financial sector money, and life company and pension fund money, in the same period. It is true that an abrupt fall in share prices in late October 1987 prompted comparisons with the Great Crash in the USA in the late 1920s, with several alarming forecasts being made of an impending slump in economic activity. An alternative view – that the stock market fall of October 1987 was due to market participants' anticipation of future inflation trouble – is, however, also tenable. If so, the likely sequel would be attempts to move portfolios away from equities and into property. In fact, the late 1980s were a period of rapid property appreciation, with 1988 seeing the peak of the house price increases and a commercial property bubble.[8]

The response of the economy to asset price gains had many similarities to the events of the Heath–Barber boom. The forecasts of a recession in 1988 were totally wrong. Domestic demand, measured in real terms, grew by 5.0 per cent in 1986 and 5.3 per cent in 1987; it then jumped by 7.9 per cent in 1988, roughly

8   Rising inflation would lead to rising interest rates. A recurrent feature of investment cycles seems to be that this anticipation of higher interest rates worries investors in equities (many of them sophisticated institutions) earlier than investors in property (many of them naive individuals). Property is often regarded as a good diversifier of investment portfolios because property returns are not correlated with equity returns.

matching the 1973 experience. In mid-1988 particularly large trade deficits were reported. Officialdom began to realise that the boom in spending was out of line with the economy's ability to produce. The boom caused a sharp fall in unemployment, and asset price inflation spread to markets in goods and services. Interest rates were raised sharply in late 1988 and 1989, with clearing bank base rates reaching 15 per cent on 5 October 1989. Higher interest rates dampened the growth of bank credit and money.[9]

The monetary data give insights into the balance-sheet strains of the period. As in 1974, money supply growth in 1990 declined while inflation (again affected by international oil prices) was rising. The result was a squeeze on real money balances and a collapse in asset values. M4 growth fell from 18.1 per cent in 1989 to 11.9 per cent in 1990 and 6.0 per cent in 1991. Company sector money – which had been soaring in 1986 and 1987 – contracted in the year to Q1 1991. The change of trend in financial sector money came later, but was more pronounced. Financial sector money dropped by 4.5 per cent (i.e. at an annualised rate of almost 9 per cent) in the first half of 1991 and showed little growth from mid-1991 to mid-1993. The imprint of these trends on pension funds' cash holdings, in particular, was marked. The pension funds had 'cash and balances with banks' of £17,492 million at end-1990, but only £9,834 million at end-1992.[10]

The main asset classes did not respond in a neat and tidy way to the change in the monetary environment. Nevertheless, the

---

9   Note that this is the first occasion on which interest rates have been introduced into the narrative. The narrative would undoubtedly have been enriched and been brought closer to reality if they had been introduced earlier, but a perfectly sensible account of events has been given without them.

10   *Financial Statistics* (London: Central Statistical Office), August 1992 issue, Table 7.22, p. 92, and December 1994 issue, Table 5.1B, p. 83.

impact of excess money until 1990 and deficient money there-after is obvious in their price movements. The equity market had reasonable years in 1988 and 1989 but struggled in 1990, and share prices in January 1991 were lower than they had been in September 1987. But a big rally in early 1991 was the start of the long bull market. By contrast, the property market was badly hit by the monetary squeeze and asset price deflation continued until 1993. The fall in house prices in the four years to mid-1993 was the worst in the UK's post-war history and scarred the financial memories of the many millions of people who had been tempted to buy a home in the boom of the late 1980s. The UK's expulsion from the Exchange Rate Mechanism of the European Monetary System in September 1992 was so humiliating that it persuaded many key policy-makers that monetary policy should in future be based on domestic conditions, not the exchange rate.

Financial sector money and asset prices in the mid- and late 1990s

The relevance of money, and in particular money held by companies and financial institutions, to asset prices is also illus-trated in the upturn of the late 1990s. Happily, the quarter-by-quarter and year-by-year variations in the strength of demand were so mild in the decade from September 1992 that a business cycle cannot readily be identified from the data. Nevertheless, the years immediately after September 1992 saw weak economic conditions. The house price collapse between 1989 and 1993 and an associated spate of bankruptcies in small businesses inflicted heavy losses on the banks, and reduced both their profits and their capital. Between 1991 and 1995 UK banks were short of capital and reluctant to expand their balance sheets. As a result, the growth of the money supply was the lowest over a sustained period since the 1950s. In the four years to end-1994 the average annual growth rate of M4 was only 5.0 per cent, dramatically lower than in the 1970s and 1980s. Domestic demand was restrained, but the economy grew satisfactorily because exports were helped by the sharp fall in the pound's value in late 1992. Inflation fell to the lowest levels for over twenty years.

But the monetary background to the economy changed once again in the mid-1990s. By late 1994 house prices had stabilised and the banks no longer needed to write off large amounts of bad mortgage loans. Moreover, by adopting new computer technologies they had reduced their costs heavily and were making good operating profits. Whereas in mid-1992 banks had been short of capital and keen to limit balance-sheet expansion, by early 1995 their capital position was comfortable and they were keen to grow at the same sort of annual rate (over 10 per cent) as seen in the 1970s and 1980s. Households were generally nervous about borrowing, because of continuing balance-sheet strain, which was a legacy of the house price collapse of the early 1990s. The banks therefore sought to expand by lending to companies, which had made a good recovery from the recession.

One difficulty was that companies did not have plans to increase investment sharply, as capacity utilisation was still below normal. Lending had therefore to be largely to finance corporate deals, such as takeovers and purchases of assets from other companies. In early 1995 the UK's biggest pharmaceutical company, Glaxo, announced that it wished to acquire another sizeable pharmaceutical company, Wellcome, in a £9 billion takeover. This was the largest-ever acquisition of one UK company by another. It was financed partly by running down Glaxo's cash balance and partly by heavy bank borrowing. In March Glaxo drew down £3.5 billion of its loan facilities in order to purchase the Wellcome shares, adding 0.5 per cent to banks' and building societies' total loan portfolios and a similar amount to M4. A series of major corporate deals followed the Glaxo–Wellcome announcement. Expenditure on mergers and acquisitions by UK companies – which had averaged just above £7 billion a year in the three years to end-1994 – was £32.1 billion in 1995. The consideration was split between £25.3 billion of cash and £6.8 billion of securities (mostly ordinary shares, but with a small element of fixed-interest securities). In turn the £25.3 billion paid both for other companies as a whole (£19.4 billion) and for the acquisition of other companies' subsidiaries (£5.8 billion). In the four years to end-1994 the stock of bank lending to companies declined from £144.2 billion to £127.8 billion; in the year to end-1995 it jumped 11.2 per cent to £142.1 billion.

The heavy volume of corporate deals in 1995 enabled the banks to achieve faster balance-sheet expansion and altered the monetary landscape. M4 growth in the year to December 1995 was 9.8 per cent, sharply higher than in the 1991–94 period. But – as in the other cyclical episodes discussed in this study – the money balances of the household sector were relatively stable. They rose by just over 7 per cent in 1995, compared with an average of just under 5 per cent a year in the previous four years. A necessary consequence was an abrupt acceleration in the growth of money held by the financial sector. Whereas in the previous four years financial sector money had risen by under 3 per cent a year, in 1995 it soared by 23.9 per cent. (Corporate sector money also increased, but by only 6.7 per cent. The effect of the merger and acquisition activity was to transfer money balances from companies to financial institutions, as the financial institutions sold shares to the bidder companies and received cash in return.)

Merger and acquisition activity remained strong over the next few years, with totals of £30.7 billion, £26.8 billion and £29.5 billion in 1996, 1997 and 1998 respectively. Bank loans were often one ingredient in the financing package. Banks were also able to expand their loans to households, as mortgage demand revived. With banks increasing their assets so easily, their deposit liabilities (i.e. money) also rose. M4 growth was 9.6 per cent in the year to December 1996, 11.8 per cent in the year to December 1997 and 8.3 per cent in the year to December 1998. But inflation stayed down, partly because shocks to the world economy (the Asian crisis in the autumn of 1997 and the Russian default in 1998) undermined commodity prices. The household sector's money balances advanced at annual rates of 6–8 per cent, beneath that of M4 as a whole. Financial sector money soared, climbing by 22.5 per cent in 1996, 26.3 per cent in 1997 and 17.5 per cent in 1998. (As in the previous episodes, the imprint of the sector-wide trend on particular classes of institution was clear. For example, life assurance companies' 'cash and balances with banks' leapt from £12.6 billion at end-1994 to £29.6 billion at end-1997.)

And, once again, we have to ask, 'What happened to asset prices?' The short answer is that the late 1990s saw a sustained bull market in equities, which reached extreme high levels of valuation. In the four successive years to December 1998 the FT All Share Index rose by 18.5 per cent, 11.7 per cent, 19.7 per cent and 10.9 per cent – 76 per cent over the whole period. Share prices continued to rise in 1999, partly in response to advances in the US stock market. In 1999, however, the monetary background in the

UK itself changed significantly. M4 growth slowed, while companies reduced their takeover activity and issued more paper (mostly in the form of bonds). The financial institutions received less cash from bids, and saw cash being depleted by the bond and equity issues. Their M4 holdings declined. The equity market peaked in December 1999. Over the next few years their money holdings grew only sluggishly, typically by 5 per cent a year or less. The equity market was unable to make much progress and at the time of writing remains lower than it was in December 1999.[11]

What was the direction of causation in the boom–bust cycles?

What do the passage of events and the statistics relating to money supply change and asset price fluctuations say about the direction of causation in the boom–bust cycles? Do they support or invalidate the arguments made by Kaldor and the narrow-money school?

A reply to the Kaldorian argument

Vital to the Kaldorian argument was the idea that banks and their customers adjusted their money holdings to 'the needs of trade'. Bank borrowing altered to keep the demand for money and the supply of money in balance. This argument runs into several difficulties, however, when an attempt is made to relate it to real-world institutions. The greater part of the money supply

---

11   The data in the discussion of the 1995–99 period were taken partly from the National Statistics website in the spring of 2004 and partly from various issues of *Financial Statistics.*

is held by members of households (i.e. the personal sector) and it is not clear that the phrase 'needs of trade' has any application to them. A high proportion of bank and building society deposits is held by people who are retired, and for them the notion of the 'needs of trade' is incongruous. More to the point for the current exercise, the Kaldorian thesis simply does not work in the UK financial sector during the boom—bust cycles. Crucially, neither of the two dominant types of financial institution – the life assurance companies and the pension funds – had any significant bank borrowings.[12] The short-term bank borrowings of these institutions were tiny relative to other balance-sheet magnitudes in the Heath—Barber and Lawson booms, and it is difficult to believe they figured centrally in management decisions.

Even more damaging for Kaldor's thesis is that bank borrowing did not change in the manner he postulated. It is obvious from Figure 7 that life offices and pension funds did not react to the receipt of extra money by repaying bank loans and thereby bringing their money holdings back to the desired level. If Kaldor were right, changes in bank loans and changes in bank deposits would have been inversely related, and the regression equation of changes in bank loans on changes in bank deposits would have had a high correlation coefficient and a regression coefficient close to minus one. An equation relating to these variables is given in an annexe to this chapter and, very plainly, it does not have these properties. The analytical sketch in Chapter 2 comes much closer to describing the task of portfolio manage-

12 This point was noted on p. 11 of Chrystal and Mizen, 'Other financial corporations: Cinderella or ugly sister?' (London: Bank of England Working Paper Series no. 151, 2001). In their words, 'Life insurance companies and pension funds, for example, hold money on deposit but they do not take on significant bank borrowings.'

Figure 7   **Does Kaldor's endogeneity thesis work in the financial sector?**
Changes in financial institutions' bank borrowings compared with changes in their money holdings, quarterly data, £m

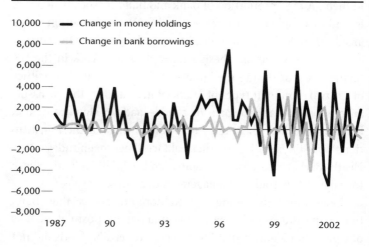

Source: Office for National Statistics website

ment in these large financial organisations. In the periods of rapid money supply growth in the boom–bust cycles the heart of this task was to maintain some sort of equilibrium between their money holdings and their total assets, when money holdings were often exploding by 10 per cent a quarter. Changes in bank borrowing hardly entered the picture. As suggested in the analytical sketch, a realistic assessment is that the senior investment executives tried to keep the money/asset ratios fairly stable. In addition in both the boom–bust cycles they became increasingly, and justifiably, worried that the value of their bond holdings would suffer from rising inflation. As they switched away from bonds, the results were surges in equity prices and commercial property values.

More generally, the problem with the Kaldorian argument is that it is cavalier in its treatment of agents at the individual level. It makes bold assertions about the macroeconomic consequences of certain actions without taking the trouble to establish a secure microeconomic underpinning for such actions. The primacy of the 'needs of trade' in financial management has obvious applicability only to the corporate sector. But – when interrogated a little – Kaldor's idea does not work even here. If a company is short of money balances, its strained liquidity is typically an aspect of balance-sheet weakness. If so, the banks are unlikely to want to lend to it. At the individual level, bank credit and the quantity of money emphatically do not adjust to 'the needs of trade'. A company on the brink of bankruptcy may need a large bank loan and its executives may plead for 'accommodation' from the local bank manager, but that does not mean it is a deserving supplicant or that it will receive finance.

In two severe corporate liquidity squeezes in our 40-year period – one in 1974, and the other in late 1990 and early 1991 – cash-starved companies could not conjure up new money balances out of thin air or even from easygoing bank managers. The only way they could restore sound balance sheets was to sell more and spend less. If they could not boost their sales revenue, they might try to offload subsidiaries, buildings, spare plots of land and other miscellaneous assets. Obviously, if other companies were also suffering from inadequate liquidity (with corporate sector money balances contracting while general inflation ran at double-digit annual rates), the efforts of numerous companies to offload subsidiaries, buildings, spare plots of land and so on would cause the prices of these assets to fall. The theme recurs, that whereas excess money balances are associated with buoyant asset prices, deficient money balances are accompanied by asset price weakness.

Alternatively, the companies might spend less, by cutting back on investment, and by economising on holdings of raw materials and components. That would certainly affect aggregate demand. If so, money was driving national expenditure, rather than the other way round. The Kaldorian argument does not fit the facts of the boom–bust cycles. The big fluctuations in aggregate money supply growth – and the associated even larger fluctuations in the money holdings of companies and financial institutions – were in no sense motivated by 'the needs of trade'. Instead they were due to the erratic, foolish and wholly exogenous mismanagement of monetary policy by the government and the Bank of England, and the results were extreme asset price volatility and the destructive boom–bust cycles.

A reply to the narrow-money school

What about the claims made by the narrow-money school and, in particular, the objections to the causal role of money made by Minford? To some extent Minford's argument is simply a misunderstanding. Of course, the assets and liabilities of financial institutions (and indeed of companies) are equal, and their net wealth is always nil. But the economy's assets must – of course – belong to someone. If a mutually owned life assurance company holds assets in the form of a large portfolio of equities, it may have liabilities to policy-holders equal to these assets and no net wealth. But that does not mean its policy-holders also have no net wealth!

On the contrary, the higher the value of the life company's assets because of, say, a soaring stock market, the higher the value of its liabilities and the better-off are the policy-holders. Despite the veil that many layers of financial intermediation may seem to draw over underlying economic realities, and despite the equivalence of financial institutions' assets and liabilities, the value of the assets they hold remains relevant to expenditure decisions.

Further, it is certainly not true that transactions within the financial system leave asset values unchanged. Minford writes as if individual agents can alter the aggregate quantity of money by switching between money balances and close alternative assets. In his discussions such switches can therefore alter the quantity of money, and so eliminate excess or deficient money holdings, without an excess supply of or demand for money affecting asset prices and the economy at large. An essential feature of the Fisher and Friedman accounts of the transmission mechanism, however, and of the sketch of asset price determination given here, is that when money is in excess supply individual attempts to reduce the quantity of money do *not* alter the aggregate quantity of money. Indeed, it was precisely this feature of the story – to repeat, the distinction between the individual and market experiments within a closed circuit of payments – which gave the quantity of money the power to determine other variables.

A fundamental feature of the analysis must be emphasised. It is essential to the argument that the quantity of money is an all-inclusive measure (i.e. a broadly defined money aggregate, which includes all bank deposits). The point is that an all-inclusive measure of money cannot be changed *in the aggregate* by individual agents' attempts to alter their own money holdings. That is the pivot on which the real balance effect works. But a narrow measure of money does not have the same characteristic. Narrow money (for example, an aggregate measure of money like M1 which includes sight deposits but not time deposits) can be changed by a large number of individual switches between sight and time deposits. Such switches do not lead to any transactions in goods, services or assets, and have no effect on the price level of goods and services or on asset prices.[13]

It is therefore surprising that Minford should prefer narrow money to broad money as a monetary indicator. Indeed, he stated his preference for the particularly limited narrow money measure Mo at the peak of the Lawson boom when asset prices were also at extreme highs. This measure excludes *all* bank deposits held by private sector agents, implying that, if contemporary money supply developments had some bearing on the asset price buoyancy, non-deposit forms of money had to be responsible. According to Minford, 'an implication of financial competition' is that 'money changes its form' and 'in particular the only "pure" money left is currency' (i.e. Mo).[14] Minford persuaded many economists at the Treasury and the Bank of England about the import-

---

13   The author has made this point on a number of occasions. See, for example, 'Credit, broad money and economic activity', in Congdon, *Reflections on Monetarism*, pp. 171–90, particularly pp. 182–3, and Tim Congdon, 'Broad money vs. narrow money', *The Review of Policy Issues* (Sheffield: Sheffield Hallam University, 1995), pp. 13–27. All measures of narrow money are endogenous in that agents' individual attempts to alter their money holdings also change the aggregate quantity of money. An all-inclusive money measure, i.e. a broad money measure, is not endogenous in this sense. A broad money measure may nevertheless be endogenous in the sense that it reflects processes within an economy, and particularly processes inside the banking system, subject to price incentives. But the endogeneity of broad money in this sense still leaves it with the ability, when disturbed from an equilibrium level, to change asset dispositions and expenditure patterns, in accordance with the Fisher/Friedman/Patinkin story.

14   Minford, *Markets Not Stakes* (London: Orion Business Books, 1998), p. 104.

ance of M0, and his analysis was one of the inputs into the policy discussion that led to the abandonment of broad money targets in the mid-1980s.

An examination of the holders of M0, however, quickly shows that it cannot have been relevant to the asset price swings seen in the boom–bust cycles. A compelling attribute of modern economies is that companies, financial institutions and wealthy individuals hold negligible amounts of notes. Part of the explanation is that notes cannot be used – without inordinate expense – to conduct the large transactions, notably transactions in substantial assets, in which companies, financial institutions and wealthy individuals are routinely involved. The irrelevance of narrow money to big corporate decisions, to the decisions that determine asset prices and influence company investment, should hardly need to be stated.

In fact, in the 40 years under consideration in this monograph no official data were compiled on the currency holdings (i.e. notes and coin) of life assurance companies and pension funds, presumably because official statisticians could not see any purpose in the exercise. Since 1987, statistics have been prepared for the currency holdings of non-monetary financial institutions, which include life assurance companies and pension funds. In 1987 they amounted to £55 million and in 2002 to £83 million. It seems likely that the bulk of this is held by minor financial institutions with some retail business involving cash, such as some hire purchase companies and pawnbrokers. For all significant financial institutions, and for all the big institutional players in UK asset markets, note holdings are trifling compared with bank deposits. A sense of perspective is given by comparing the bank deposits held by non-monetary (i.e. non-bank, non-building-society) financial institutions with their currency holdings (see Table 4). At the end of 2002 the deposits – at £279,597 million – were almost 3,400 times larger than the amount of currency. For life assurance companies and pension funds by themselves, the multiple would have been considerably higher, but – as noted – official data are not available.

Minford appears to believe that the variations in the growth rate of broad money were unrelated to the extreme asset price movements of the boom–bust cycles. This monograph has shown that the broad money growth rates of 20 per cent a year in the boom were associated with both 40 per cent, 50 per cent and 60 per cent annual growth rates of money held by the financial sector as whole, and 40 per cent, 50 per cent and 60 per cent annual growth rates of money held by such leading institutions as life offices and pension funds. Equally, it has shown that the decelerations in broad money growth rates to 10 per cent a year or less during the busts were associated with virtual stagnation in the money holdings of the financial sector and leading financial institutions. It is clear that the periods in which the institutions' money holdings were expanding rapidly were also periods of rising asset prices and that the periods when they were static were periods of falling asset prices. Further, the notion that financial institutions' senior executives cared more about their note holdings (i.e. their Mo balances) than about their bank deposits is – to say the least – most implausible, given the quantitative insignificance of the note holdings. Minford wants us to believe that 'monetary forces' are best represented by 'the printing of money' and 'Mo', and that such variables 'are still central to our understanding of inflation'. Some economists apparently attach credence to these remarks, but it is difficult to believe that Mo

Table 4 **The insignificance of financial institutions' currency holdings**

	Non-monetary financial institutions' holdings of:		Multiple of deposits held to currency held
	Sterling deposits £m	Currency £m	
1987	40,082	55	729
1988	51,008	59	865
1989	73,142	63	1,161
1990	86,210	70	1,232
1991	77,117	74	1,042
1992	88,140	77	1,145
1993	99,866	79	1,264
1994	106,180	81	1,311
1995	144,709	83	1,743
1996	173,317	83	2,088
1997	200,529	83	2,416
1998	216,459	83	2,608
1999	200,617	83	2,417
2000	247,853	83	2,986
2001	286,958	83	3,457
2002	279,597	83	3,369

Source: National Statistics website

could ever have been central to the asset price inflation that was such a notorious element in the boom–bust cycles.[15]

What about other views of the narrow-money school? According to Walters, 'one would clearly not count £50,000 negotiable CDs [or 'certificates of deposit'] as money; so far as I am aware no one would ever accept such an instrument to pay an outstanding expense'.[16] But – when applied to corporate entities and, in particular, to large financial institutions – Walters' comment ignores the practicalities of the matter. A life assurance company would be foolish to keep its money in a cash till,

15   Ibid., p. 105.
16   Walters, *Britain's Economic Renaissance*, pp. 116–17.

because of the awkwardness and inefficiency of making large asset transactions in notes. But it would also be unwise to leave its money in a non-interest-bearing sight deposit (or 'checkable account', in Walters' terminology), as it would fail to collect the interest on quite sizeable sums of policy-holder funds. Its appropriate behaviour would be to hold money in an interest-bearing but highly liquid form, such as in £50,000 parcels of CDs. Because of its bargaining power (as a large customer) with the banks, a life assurance company can convert a £50,000 CD into a checkable account at little cost and use the funds in purchases of equities, buildings, land and so on. Walters' conception of 'money in the transactions sense' as 'money readily available for small-scale, retail transactions' is limited and unsatisfactory. In a modern economy money is used in all transactions, small, medium and large, while the majority of transactions *in assets* are so large that they can be conducted sensibly only by payment instructions against bank deposits.[17] When asset-rich agents take decisions to alter their portfolios, the critical definition of money to them is a broadly defined one, in which deposits are dominant. Their decisions on the right balance between all their non-monetary

---

17 In an article on 'Monetary policy, gilts and equities' in the December 1970 issue of *The Investment Analyst*, Walters analysed the link between the money supply and share prices and remarked, 'My predilection is to believe that movements in the money stock are the *cause* of the oscillations in the equity market'. (The paper was republished in John Goodchild and Clive Callow [eds], *Double Takes* [Chichester: John Wiley, 2000]. The quotation is from p. 101 of this book.) But it is difficult to believe that any narrow money measure could cause equity market fluctuations, for the reasons given in the text here. In fact, Walters was critical of the explosion in the growth rate of *broad money* in the boom of the early 1970s, and saw a connection then between the high rates of *broad money growth* and large asset price increases. In a footnote on p. 118 of *Britain's Economic Renaissance* he notes that he used 'M3 statistics' to make an accurate prediction of 15 per cent inflation in 1974, where M3 was a broad money measure.

assets and all their money assets are far more interesting for the wider economy than their decisions on the right balance between different types of monetary instrument (such as £50,000 CDs, term deposits and interest-bearing sight deposits) within an all-inclusive money total.[18]

Annexe

The Kaldorian thesis is that bank borrowings change to eliminate an excess supply of or demand for money: so an excess supply of or demand for money does not alter expenditure patterns. In other words, the change in bank loans should be similar (i.e. with a regression coefficient in an estimated equation close to one) to the recent or concurrent change in cash and deposits, with the sign reversed.

Data on the net acquisition of financial assets are available, on a quarterly basis, for 'insurance corporations and pension funds' from 1987, including three categories, 'Currency and deposits' and 'Short-term loans' (from MFIs [or 'monetary financial institutions', mostly banks]), in both sterling and foreign currency. Note that changes in borrowing in foreign currency were large relative to those in sterling in the period under consideration, but no significant relationship could be identified with any definition of bank borrowing. (The series were NBSG, NBWX and NBXB in

---

18 The survey of asset price movements in the UK in this chapter was influenced by the work of Gordon Pepper, senior partner of the stockbroking firm W. Greenwell & Co. from 1980 to 1986 and later professor at City University Business School. See, for example, pp. 203–9 of Pepper, *Money, Credit and Asset Prices* (Basingstoke and London: Macmillan, 1994), where share price movements are attributed to deviations of the growth rate of broad money from that of nominal GDP.

the 2004 National Statistics database.) The following relationship is found between changes in bank loans and changes in currency and deposits:

Change in bank loans, £m per quarter = £138.2 million − 0.011 (change in currency and deposits, £m in same quarter)

The following statistics are derived from the regression:

r squared	0.0006
Standard error for intercept term	140.25
Standard error of regression coefficient	0.05
t statistic for intercept term	0.99
t statistic for regression coefficient	−0.21

The regression coefficient is not significantly different from zero, while the relationship itself has a very poor fit (with an r^2 of almost nothing), and neither the intercept term nor the regression coefficient is statistically significant, with very low values of the t statistics.

As far as UK financial institutions in the period from 1987 to 2003 are concerned, the Kaldorian thesis of the endogeneity of money can be rejected outright.

4 MONEY AND ASSET PRICES IN THE AMERICAN GREAT DEPRESSION AND CONTEMPORARY JAPAN

The linkages between money and asset prices in the UK's cycles in the second half of the twentieth century can be easily traced, partly because of the abundance of data and the continuity of the institutional framework. What about other well-known examples of marked asset price volatility and associated macroeconomic instability? Can the same sort of analytical approach be harnessed and put to work? Because of their prominence in debates between economists, this chapter will look at two episodes – the Great Depression in the USA between 1929 and 1993, and the asset bubble and subsequent prolonged macroeconomic malaise in Japan from the mid-1980s to today.

Money and asset prices in the USA, 1929–33

The Great Depression in the USA in the four years from 1929 was the most cataclysmic economic event in US history. Share prices collapsed and industrial production halved, causing millions of people to lose their jobs and inflicting hardship on many of those who remained in employment. The severity and apparently arbitrary character of this disaster blighted the reputation of market capitalism for at least a generation. Much has already been written about the Great Depression, although no agreement has been reached on the pattern of cause and effect. A classic analysis was provided by Friedman and Schwartz in their 1963 study, *A Monetary History of the United States, 1867–1960*. Their argument was that the dominant causal influence on 'the Great Contraction' (as they termed it) was the fall in the money supply. On their favoured measure of money (currency held by the public plus all deposits in commercial banks) this fall – on a peak to trough basis – was of almost 40 per cent, from $48.2 billion in October 1929 to $29.7 billion in April 1933. They blamed the ineptitude of Federal Reserve policy in these years, with 'the financial collapse' resulting 'from the shift of power [within the Federal Reserve system] from New York to the other Federal Reserve banks'.[1]

An academic debate has developed about the relative importance of the money supply decline and the stock market collapse in the economic downturn. Friedman and Schwartz's assessment was nuanced. They saw the stock market crash as 'a symptom of the underlying forces making for a severe contraction in economic activity', but also accorded it a causal role in making consumers and business enterprises more cautious. One effect was on 'desired balance sheets', with shifts 'away from stocks and toward bonds' and 'away from securities of all kinds and toward money holdings'. As a result the velocity of money fell and 'the stock market crash made the decline in income sharper than it would otherwise have been'.[2] Nevertheless, their emphasis was on the money supply, not share prices, as having the primary role in the USA's economic trauma in the early 1930s.

Other strongly stated positions in the debate are represented by Galbraith and Kindleberger, on the one hand, and Meltzer,

---

[1]   Milton Friedman and Anna Schwartz, *A Monetary History of the United States, 1867–1960* (Princeton, NJ: Princeton University Press, 1963), p. 419.

[2]   Ibid., pp. 306–7.

on the other. Galbraith's celebrated *The Great Crash* and Kindleberger's *The World in Depression 1929–39* both argued that the slump in share prices was an independent causal influence on business activity. In Kindleberger's words, 'It is hard to avoid [the conclusion] that there is something to the conventional wisdom that characterised the crash as the start of the process.'[3] Against this, Meltzer affirmed in his *A History of the Federal Reserve* that the actions of the Federal Reserve – and in particular, its failure to expand the monetary base sufficiently – were to blame for the slump. Like Friedman and Schwartz, he put money at the centre of the story.

The contrast between a money-supply and a share-price explanation may be misleading, however. It might be better to see share prices as among the asset prices that are determined, to a large extent, by monetary forces. The stock market crash then becomes not an alternative explanation of the Great Depression, but part of an expanded monetary account of events. This shift of interpretation becomes convincing if the monetary aggregate under consideration is not narrow money (as in Meltzer's work), but a wider money measure which includes time deposits (as in Friedman and Schwartz's *Monetary History*). The advantages of a wider money measure ought to be clear in the context of portfolio decisions. Wealth-holders in the USA in the 1920s and the 1930s – just like wealth-holders in Britain in the second half of the twentieth century – had a choice between any of the following assets:

---

3   Charles Kindleberger, *The World in Depression, 1929–39* (Berkeley: University of California Press, revised edn, 1986), p. 116, and quoted on p. 255 of Allan Meltzer, *A History of the Federal Reserve* (Chicago and London: University of Chicago Press, 2003), vol. I.

- cash, in the sense of notes and coin;
- demand deposits;
- time deposits;
- financial securities; and
- tangible assets.

Bluntly, time deposits cannot be deleted from the list of assets. For monetary economists to concentrate only on cash and demand deposits (i.e. the M1 money measure, more or less), or even on cash itself, is bizarre. It is true that in the 1920s and 1930s US citizens held a far higher ratio of currency to time deposits than today. Indeed, the money holdings of poor people, without bank accounts, would have been dominated by currency. But these would not have been the people whose behaviour influenced asset prices or was most critical in the determination of economic activity. Significant wealth-holders – then, as now – would have been balancing at the margin their holdings of money *in the form of time deposits* against their holdings of non-monetary assets, including all financial securities. (In the portfolios of the very wealthy – the top 5 per cent of the population who owned the bulk of the US stock market – currency was a tiny proportion of total wealth.) Logically, the level of time deposits – not the level of currency and demand deposits – was the monetary variable most relevant to the stock market. To exclude time deposits from a causal position in the analysis – as in Meltzer's work – is to overlook the leading actor in the drama; it is the equivalent in monetary history of playing Hamlet without the Prince.[4]

---

4   Friedman and Schwartz are much friendlier towards the broad money aggregates than Meltzer. On p. 630 of *A Monetary History* they say 'currency held by the public plus demand *and time deposits* ... in commercial banks' (author's italics) is 'our

Fortunately, a large body of data is available to throw light on the points at issue. The main difficulty with supporters of narrow money measures is that the monetary base did *not* contract in the Great Depression. Embarrassingly for their position, the public's holdings of currency were much higher in March 1933 (at the nadir of the depression) than in October 1929 (when the stock market had its first big tumble). (In figures the public's currency holdings were $3,832 million in October 1929 and $5,509 million in March 1933.)[5] The rise in note holdings was a response to the insecurity of bank deposits, as thousands of banks failed and were unable to repay creditors (including their depositors) in full. Although the Federal Reserve could undoubtedly have done more to counter the deflationary pressures, it did print more notes and expand its balance sheet. The expansion of its operations – which occurred through very large purchases of securities – was in accordance with the textbook

concept of money'. This appears to be a clear-cut endorsement of broad money. A footnote discussion on pp. 649–50, however, is more equivocal. 'The … criterion for choosing the total [i.e. the money aggregate] to which to apply the term "money" is by no means clearly appropriate … It must depend on the purpose and on the empirical relevance of a particular distinction for that purpose under specific circumstances, which is to say, on the empirical stability and regularity of relationships between the chosen total and other variables.' Friedman and Schwartz are therefore inclined to favour broad money measures, but are flexible in their attitude. (Keynes's views on this question were close to those of Friedman and Schwartz. After defining 'the rate of interest' as 'what can be obtained for parting with control over … money in exchange for a debt' on p. 267 of the main text of *The General Theory*, Keynes added a footnote to the effect that 'Without disturbance to this definition, we can draw the line between "money" and "debt" at whatever point is most convenient for handling a particular problem … It is often convenient in practice to include in *money* time-deposits with banks and, occasionally, even such instruments as (*e.g.*) treasury bills. As a rule, I shall, as in my *Treatise on Money*, assume that money is co-extensive with deposits.')

5   Friedman and Schwartz, *Monetary History*, pp. 712–13.

maxims of central banking, even though it was on an insufficient scale.[6]

The trouble lay rather in the commercial banking system and particularly in the decline in bank deposits, as banks suffered losses and called in loans because of the depletion of their capital. As they called in loans, both their assets and deposit liabilities decreased. With interest rates falling and their profits disappearing, the banks were unable to keep paying interest on time deposits. (They had been paying such interest extensively in the prosperous late 1920s.) Time deposits therefore became less attractive and fell more steeply than demand deposits. But, as has been mentioned, wealthy individuals, the kind of individuals who would have held large securities portfolios, were balancing time deposits against common stocks in their overall asset holdings. As their holdings of time deposits went down, their money balances became too small relative to their other assets. (They suffered from 'an excess demand for money', in the terminology of Chapter 2.) As individuals they sold other assets (especially common stocks), believing that thereby they might rebuild an equilibrium money holding. But, as explained in Chapter 2, sales of securities

---

6   This is not to deny that yet greater expansion of the Federal Reserve's balance sheet, and still further enlargement of the monetary base, would have helped economic activity. But the Federal Reserve had to worry about the quality of the assets it would purchase if it embarked on headlong expansion. Keynes saw the point in a visit to Chicago in 1931. At a conference organised by the Harris Foundation Institute, he remarked that 'When the Federal Reserve System buys governments, it means the public has increased deposits, and they can't afford to accumulate non-interest-bearing assets beyond a certain point. But it does mean the scale of operations may be *rather uncomfortably large* in order to produce consequences' (Johnson and Moggridge [eds], *Collected Writings of Keynes*, vol. XX, *Activities 1929–31: Rethinking Employment and Unemployment Policies* [London and Basingstoke: Macmillan Press for the Royal Economic Society, 1981], p. 533, author's italics).

Figure 8   **Stock prices and time deposits in the USA, 1920–35**
Quarterly data, levels, index values and $bn

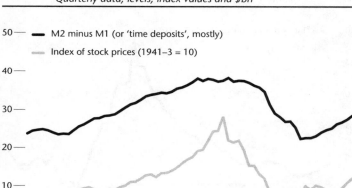

Source: Nathan Balke and Robert J. Gordon, 'Appendix B: Historical Data', especially pp. 803–4, in R. J. Gordon (ed.), *The American Business Cycle: Continuity and Change* (Chicago and London: University of Chicago Press, 1986)

by any one agent do not increase the aggregate amount of money. Instead they reduce the money balances held by the counterpart buyers of the securities and leave the aggregate amount of money unchanged.

Since, in fact, the aggregate amount of money was contracting in the early 1930s because of the crisis in the banking system, virtually all wealth-holders wanted to sell common stocks. But – within a closed circuit of traders – they could sell only to each other. Plainly, equilibrium required that stock prices go down. As the wider macroeconomic environment was hostile to profits, stocks fell far more than either national income or the money supply

Figure 9 **Stock prices and the monetary base in the USA, 1920–35**
Quarterly data, levels, index values and $bn

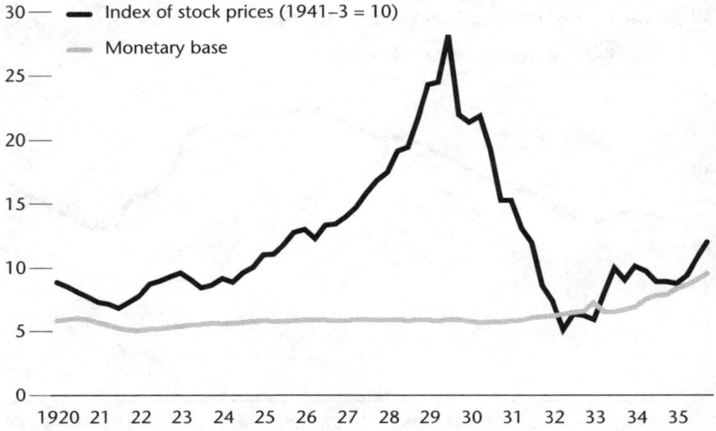

Source: Nathan Balke and Robert J. Gordon, 'Appendix B: Historical Data', especially pp. 803–4, in R. J. Gordon (ed.), *The American Business Cycle: Continuity and Change* (Chicago and London: University of Chicago Press, 1986)

(however measured). Nevertheless, the stock market crash was part of a general weakness in asset prices which was attributable to the decline in the money supply. The accompanying Figures 8 and 9 compare the level of the stock market, first, with that of time deposits (where there is a clear correlation) and, second, with the monetary base (where there is no correlation whatsoever).

Asset prices – and of course the egregious behaviour of the stock market – must be integrated into a convincing analysis of the Great Depression. To suggest that asset price movements of the 1930s need to be set within a monetary context is hardly radical, since that was the thrust of the leading innovations in economic theory during the decade. Quite apart from Keynes's insistence in *The General Theory* on what he termed 'the speculative demand for money' (i.e. the demand to hold money in order to improve the timing of bond purchases), Hicks proposed in his well-known essay of 1935 on 'A suggestion for simplifying the theory of money' that 'What has to be explained is the decision to hold assets in the form of barren money, rather than of interest- or profit-yielding securities.'[7] Asset price developments must be related not just to a sub-set of monetary assets, such as the monetary base or narrow money, but to an all-inclusive money measure including time deposits. This study does not have the space to elaborate the precise connections – month by month, institution by institution, and stock market operator by stock market operator – between the total amount of bank deposits and the behaviour of the US stock market between 1929 and 1933. Nevertheless, the message of the charts is striking. The asset price collapses in the USA in the Great Depression can be interpreted as a by-product of the fall in time deposits and have no clear connection with the monetary base, while the monetary aggregate with the greatest power to explain events must be a broadly defined one (i.e. M2 rather than M1 or the base).

Money and asset prices in the Japanese bubble and later malaise 1985–2003

The late 1980s were years of great speculative excitement in Japan. After almost forty years of exceptionally rapid economic growth, Japan's economy had become the second largest in the world.

---

7   Sir John Hicks, *Critical Essays in Monetary Theory* (Oxford: Oxford University Press), p. 66.

Indeed, books were written about the possibility that its output might overtake the USA's within the next twenty years and that the 21st century would be characterised by Japanese leadership of the world economy. Amid this euphoria, stock market and real estate prices rose relentlessly. At the end of 1989 the Nikkei stock index was six times higher than it had been a decade earlier. The second half of the decade was the most extreme, with the Nikkei index showing a compound annual rate of increase of over 31 per cent in the four years from the end of 1985. Corporate equity became exceptionally overvalued. In the mid-1970s the price/earnings ratio of equities in the Tokyo Stock Exchange's first section had been in line with the typical long-run average in most countries of about 15; in the late 1980s the comparable figure was 60 or 70. As in the USA in the late 1920s, the upward rush in share prices was not accompanied by marked macroeconomic imbalance. The current account of the balance of payments was in continual surplus, while the wholesale price index was at much the same level in 1990 as it had been five years earlier.

Policy-makers were concerned, however, that equity market overvaluation was leading to resource misallocation and corruption in the financial system, and decided that asset prices had to be brought down. Their determination to tighten policy was reinforced in the summer of 1990 by Iraq's invasion of Kuwait, which prompted a sharp rise in oil prices and threatened Japan's price stability. The Bank of Japan's discount rate – which had been only 2.5 per cent in 1987 and 1988 – was raised in a sequence of steps to reach 6 per cent in the autumn of 1990. The Nikkei index slithered from a peak of almost 40,000 in late 1989 to less than half that level in 1992 and continued to fall in later years. With asset prices in retreat, both consumer confidence and corporate spending became chronically weak. The Japanese economy entered a prolonged malaise of semi-stagnation which lasted until the opening years of the 21st century.

So much is well known and familiar. As usual, it has been possible to tell the story in terms of central bank actions and interest rates, and without any reference to the quantity of money. Indeed, economists at the Bank of Japan – like their counterparts at the Bank of England – have described 'the transmission mechanism of monetary policy' as pivoting on the interest rate set by the central bank in the money markets.[8] However, the behaviour of the money aggregates illuminates the passage of events and identifies key causal influences in asset price determination. To restrict the discussion to interest rates, and the presumed effects of interest rates on expenditure, is to provide an incomplete and unsatisfactory account of events. The implicit view is that the economy consists only of monetary base assets and the goods and services that comprise national expenditure. This is simply wrong. The economy also includes sight and time deposits, and a wide

8   A paper on 'One year under "quantitative easing"' by Masaaki Shirakawa was published by the Bank of Japan's Institute for Monetary and Economic Studies in 2002 (IMES Discussion Paper Series 2002-E-3, April 2002). On p. 35 it presented a figure on 'The standard transmission mechanism of monetary policy'. Arrows connect a box, 'Change in reserves', to another box, 'Change in short-term interest rates', to yet another, 'Changes in the prices of financial assets (i.e., medium- and long-term interest rates, foreign exchange rates, stock prices, etc.)', and then, both directly and via another box, 'Change in the behaviour of financial institutions', to the final box, 'Change in the behaviour of domestic private economic agents, such as firms and households and also overseas economic agents'. The approach was similar to that of the paper prepared in 1999 by the Monetary Policy Committee of the Bank of England for the attention of the Treasury Committee of the House of Commons. A vital attribute of macroeconomic equilibrium – that the quantity of money be willingly held at the prevailing levels of asset prices and national income – was ignored by both the Bank of Japan and the Bank of England.

variety of financial and tangible assets, while wealth-holders had at all times to seek the most favourable balance between monetary and non-monetary assets in their portfolios.

For most of the post-war period Japan's banks had been highly profitable and were able, even after paying dividends, to expand their capital and balance sheets at annual rates of up to 20 per cent or more. Annual rates of money supply growth in the 1960s and 1970s were typically around 15 to 25 per cent. (The concept of money here and later is the 'M2 plus certificates of deposit' measure, unless otherwise specified.) More moderate rates of under 10 per cent were recorded in the early 1980s. This could be attributed to a wider slowdown in the trend rate of output growth and a narrowing of profit margins throughout the economy, including the banking system. As Japan had caught up with Western technologies, it could not achieve rapid output growth merely by imitation. But in 1986, partly under pressure from American policy-makers worried about the weakness of the dollar, the Japanese government agreed to ease monetary policy. The Bank of Japan's discount rate of 2.5 per cent in 1987 and 1988 stimulated the demand for bank credit, and was accompanied by annual rates of money supply growth in the low double digits.

In the year to end-1989 the money supply increased by 12.0 per cent, plainly excessive relative to the economy's trend rate of output growth. In 1990 higher interest rates deterred bank credit and the growth of money slowed to 7.4 per cent. The decline in money growth in 1991 was even more pronounced, and in the three years to end-1991, end-1992 and end-1993, the rates of change in the money supply were 2.3 per cent, −0.2 per cent and 2.2 per cent. The fall in the annual rate of money growth – from a double-digit figure in 1989 to virtual stagnation less than three years later

– was one of the sharpest changes in the pace of monetary expansion in Japan's post-1945 experience.

Of course, these were also the years in which the stock market bubble burst and the long malaise of asset price weakness began. The stock market gyrations in Japan in the late 1980s and early 1990s seem as amenable to explanation in terms of the quantity of money as they are to explanation in terms of central bank action on interest rates. Is it possible to say more about the types of agent most involved in asset price determination, echoing the discussion in the previous chapter of the role of financial institutions and companies in the UK? Japanese statistics on money and banking are detailed and extensive, but not surprisingly they are prepared differently from those in other industrial countries. Data are, however, published in the Bank of Japan's *Economic Statistics Annual* on the M1 and quasi-money holdings of 'private enterprises' and 'individuals'. The category 'private enterprises' includes financial institutions, although money held by industrial and commercial companies would have predominated in the 1980s. As it happens, companies' purchases of equity in other companies were a particularly important feature of the Japanese financial scene in those years. The purpose was to establish share 'cross-holdings' which would hinder takeover activity and entrench existing managements. (The author has not been able to obtain statistics that further differentiate money held by non-bank financial institutions *as a whole* from the money held by private enterprises, although abundant balance-sheet information is available for various categories of financial institution.)

Figure 10 compares annual changes in the Nikkei index with annual changes in private enterprises' quasi-money between 1980 and 1993. 'Quasi-money' consists of all deposits minus demand

Figure 10 **Money, and the boom and bust in the Japanese stock market, 1980–93**

Annual % changes in Nikkei index, against right-hand axis, and quasi-money (i.e., time deposits) held by private enterprises, against left-hand axis

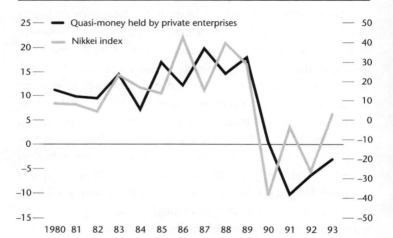

Source: Bank of Japan

deposits, and corresponds more or less to time deposits in the definitions of North American and European countries. The two series did not match up exactly every year from 1980 to 1993, but the rough parallelism of their movement is obvious. Broadly speaking, when companies' holdings of time deposits were rising, so also were share prices; when companies' holdings of time deposits were falling, so also were share prices. Changes in share prices were generally twice as large as changes in companies' time deposits. A fair comment is that – as in the USA in the 1930s, and as in the UK during the boom–bust cycles – the behaviour of money, particularly in the form of time deposits in corporate hands, was a crucial influence on the vicissitudes of the stock market. Further, an attempt to explain asset prices by means of narrow money measures is untenable.[9] In Japan, as in every other major industrial economy, significant wealth-holders have to balance *all* their money holdings (i.e an all-inclusive money measure) against non-monetary assets in portfolios where notes and coin often do not figure at all. The notion that the monetary base has any direct relevance to asset markets is as thorough a misunderstanding of the institutional realities of modern Japan as it is of the institutional realities of modern Britain.

In the mid- and late 1990s Japan was unable to shake off the macroeconomic malaise that had begun with the bursting of the bubble. Asset price weakness caused a high incidence of bad loans and loan write-offs in the banking system. With the banks short of capital, they were unable to expand their balance sheets. Money supply growth – which had routinely been over 20 per cent a year in the 1960s – fell to very low rates of 2 or 3 per cent a year. In the five years to 1998 the average annual increase in M2 plus CDs was 3.1 per cent; in the five years to 2003 it was only 2.7 per cent. Asset prices remained weak, with land prices (crucial to banks' loan collateral) falling every year in the decade to 2003. The economy

---

9   The author carried out econometric tests on the relationship between changes in different money aggregates and changes in share prices in Japan from 1980 to 1993 (the period of the Japanese share price boom and bust). The equation tested took the form *Change in Nikkei index, % p.a.* = α + β *(Change in 'money', % p.a.)* for various definitions of money. There was a reasonable link between broader definitions of money and share prices and no link between narrow definitions of money and share prices. The detailed results can be obtained from the author.

had only brief and fitful recoveries, and the price level fell slightly in the early years of the 21st century.

This period is of considerable interest to economic theory as it provided a laboratory experiment on the relative importance of narrow and broad measures of money, and of money and credit. A standard prescription of visiting US economists in the late 1990s was that the Bank of Japan should expand the monetary base (typically by large purchases of government bonds, but sometimes by purchases of foreign exchange), in the expectation that the banks would respond to their excess base holdings by increasing their earning assets. Some economists thought that a faster rate of increase in the monetary base *by itself* or in the M1 narrow money measure would be sufficient to secure recovery;[10] others believed that the purpose of the exercise was to stimulate the banks to make more loans and that extra bank credit, again *by itself*, would be the vital new development.[11] In 2001, 2002 and 2003 the Bank

10 Belief in the therapeutic powers of basing policy on the monetary base is associated with the American economist Ben McCallum. See his 'Specification and analysis of monetary policy rule for Japan', *Monetary and Economic Studies* (Bank of Japan, November 1993), vol. 11, pp. 1–45. As in his *History of the Federal Reserve*, an account of monetary policy-making in the USA in the first half of the twentieth century, Meltzer favours tracking the monetary base and the M1 measure of money when analysing macroeconomic developments in modern Japan. He believes that the central bank should operate on the monetary base to influence M1. In some of his papers he equates 'monetary expansion' with 'expansion of the monetary base'. See, for example, the note 'Comment on Japan and the Asian financial crisis' on his research website, www.gsia.cmu.edu/afs/andrew/gsia/meltzer.

11 References to a supposed link between bank lending and 'spending' proliferate in newspapers and business magazines. The lack of a rigorous theoretical basis for such a link is discussed in Chapter 5 of this study. For a more heavyweight contribution suffering from the same misunderstanding, see Glenn Hoggarth and Joe Thomas, 'Will bank recapitalisation boost domestic demand in Japan?', *Financial Stability Review* (London: Bank of England), June 1999 issue. In the opening paragraph 'a cut-back in lending' is bracketed with 'reducing spending by the household and corporate sectors'.

of Japan responded to these calls by a conscious policy of 'quant-itative easing', making enormous purchases of not only govern-ments bonds but also Treasury and Financing bills (short-dated instruments issued by the Ministry of Finance). Banks' reserve balances jumped from 5.5 trillion yen at the end of 2000 to 27.8 trillion yen at the end of 2003. The impact on the monetary base and M1 money measures was palpable. Indeed, in 2002 M1 soared by 27.6 per cent, more than in any year in the 1980s or 1990s. But the broader measures of money were little affected. They continued to plod forward at the 2–3 per cent annual rates seen for most of the 1990s.

Table 5 summarises the behaviour of the main money measures in the five years to end-2003, and compares them with the rate of increase in real domestic demand. (Nominal domestic demand often fell, with the domestic demand deflator being negative on average by about 1.5 per cent a year.) The macroeconomic inef-fectiveness of the surges in the monetary base and M1 is obvious.[12]

---

12 This is not to deny that increases in the monetary base would have worked in Japan *if they had been on a sufficiently large scale to raise the growth rate of an all-inclusive measure of money.* In the extreme the central bank could have made asset purchases (of bonds, equities or whatever) from non-bank agents equal to 10, 20 or 30 per cent of GDP and paid for them with notes. If the notes had then been deposited with the commercial banks, the monetary effect would be the same as if the banks had purchased the assets from non-banks. But the location of risk in the banking system would be different in the two cases. If the central bank pur-chased the assets and issued notes to pay for them, the commercial banks would receive the notes as the asset matching the deposits and these extra assets would be claims on the central bank. The risk that the bonds, equities and so on might fall in value would therefore lie with the central bank. On the other hand, if the commercial banks bought assets from non-banks and paid for them by crediting sums to deposits, the risk of falling asset values would lie with the commercial banks. The possibility of severe losses on the assets it acquires can be a constraint on large-scale expansionary open market operations by a central bank. Whether this risk of loss ought to constrain the central bank is a matter of debate. The

Excess base and excess holdings of sight deposits did *not* help asset prices or stimulate economic activity; instead they led to shifts in the relative sizes of the components of a broad money measure (i.e. because of transfers of money between different types of deposit), but such shifts were of no significance to the wider economy. By contrast, the changes in the money supply (on the standard M2 plus CDs definition) and broadly defined liquidity were in the same ballpark as the changes in private domestic demand. No one knows what would have happened if official action had instead been focused on raising the growth rates of broad money, but it is plain that the persisting low growth rates of broad money were accompanied by further asset price disappointment and negligible increases in nominal GDP.[13]

What about bank credit? In the early and mid-1990s Japan's banks took a lenient attitude towards borrowers who could not repay, or even service, their loans, hoping that with the return of better times the quality of the loans would improve. They added interest to loan principals, even if there was little likelihood of the

---

author is grateful to Milton Friedman and Allan Meltzer for an exchange of e-mails that helped to clarify his thinking on the topic.

13   As noted earlier in Chapter 2, Krugman claimed in *The Return of Depression Economics* that Japan was in a liquidity trap in the late 1990s (pp. 70–77). Since the central bank discount rate was already at zero, it was obviously true that the central bank could not drive interest rates lower by expansionary open market purchases. But Krugman was writing about only one kind of trap (which might be termed 'the narrow trap'), that which arises when *the short-term interest rate in the money markets cannot be reduced by increases in the monetary base*. Keynes's own trap was different. It arose when *increases in the broadly defined quantity of money could not reduce the yield on government bonds* and might be called 'the broad trap'. Since the rates of growth of broad money stayed very low in Japan throughout the prolonged malaise, no one knows whether it suffered from Keynes's liquidity trap. (The author distinguished between the narrow and broad liquidity traps in two research papers in the March 2003 and April 2003 issues of Lombard Street Research's *Monthly Economic Review*.)

Table 5 **Growth rates of different money concepts and private domestic demand in Japan, 1999–2003, % p.a.**

	Banks' cash reserves	Monetary base	M1	M2 plus CDs	Broadly defined liquidity	Private domestic demand
1999	23.6	44.5	10.5	3.6	3.3	0.8
2000	−5.9	−19.9	8.2	2.1	3.1	2.8
2001	36.8	19.4	8.5	2.8	2.5	−0.6
2002	155.2	11.8	27.6	3.3	0.5	0.4
2003	51.4	12.0	8.2	1.7	0.6	2.4

Note: Figures for cash reserves are average of year. Otherwise data relate to year-end, except those for domestic demand, which are for whole year.

borrowers' early financial rehabilitation. The loan assets of Japan's domestically licensed banks therefore rose from 435.7 trillion yen at end-1991 to 475.7 trillion yen at end-1997, with a compound annual rate of increase of 1.5 per cent. But after the announcement of a 'Big Bang' of financial reform by Prime Minister Hashimoto in November 1996 the banks took a more robust line and began to write off bad loans. From the end of 1997 to the end of 2003 the loan assets of Japan's domestically licensed banks fell from 475.7 trillion yen to 407.1 trillion yen, with a compound annual rate of decline of 2.6 per cent. If bank credit *by itself* were critical to the behaviour of the economy, a fair expectation would be that these six years would be significantly worse for asset prices and domestic demand than the previous six.

In fact, Japanese macroeconomic conditions in the six years to end-2003 were much the same as in the six years to end-1997. Share prices had their ups and downs, but their average rate of decline in the later six-year period was less than in the earlier. The rate of growth in private domestic demand was a shade higher in the earlier period (0.8 per cent a year) than in the later period (0.2

per cent a year), but the difference was trifling. Non-residential investment – which some economists might expect to be particularly sensitive to 'credit conditions' – was slightly stronger in the later period than in the earlier. In short, the change in the trend of bank credit after Hashimoto's Big Bang had minimal effect on key economic variables.

The Japanese economy's ability to shrug off the bank credit contraction from 1997 stemmed from the relative stability of monetary growth. As in the USA during and after the Great Depression, the critical financial variable for the economy was neither the behaviour of bank credit alone nor the composition of banks' assets, but the quantity of money. Banks compensated for the decline in their loan assets by increasing their holdings of securities, particularly government bonds. Japan's domestically licensed banks' holdings of government bonds more than trebled from under 30 trillion yen at the end of 1996 to over 90 trillion yen at the end of 2003. The expansion in their government bond holdings was roughly similar in size to the contraction in their loan assets. As a result the shrinkage of loan portfolios did not lead to a decline in total assets or, on the other side of the balance sheet, to a fall in deposit liabilities. In fact, the money supply still grew in these years, even if only slowly. Arguably, policy-makers could have been more deliberate and aggressive in offering government bond issues that would have been attractive to the banks, and so encouraging them to expand their balance sheets and deposit liabilities more rapidly.[14]

---

14 The author advocated large-scale purchases of *long-dated* government bonds *from non-banks by the government itself* in order directly to increase the quantity of *broad* money in an article in *Central Banking* in 2002 (see Tim Congdon, 'What is to be done about Japan's financial crisis?', *Central Banking*, vol. 12, no. 4, May 2002, pp. 67–72).

The larger lesson of the Japanese malaise is that traditional monetary theory provides correct insights into the determination of both asset prices and national income. As that theory recognises, full macroeconomic equilibrium requires that the quantity of money – broadly defined to include all money balances – be willingly held at prevailing levels of asset prices and national income. So the behaviour of the quantity of money must be monitored, both to help businessmen and investors in the interpretation of the economic scene, and to guide policy-makers towards the right decisions. Neither a sub-set of monetary assets (i.e. the monetary base or M1) nor bank credit alone has given reliable signals to the cyclical fluctuations and asset price instabilities experienced by the Japanese economy since the mid-1980s.

5 CREDIT, EXPENDITURE AND ASSET PRICES

The purpose of this study has been to demonstrate the importance of money, based on broad definitions, to asset prices and economic activity (and ultimately to the price level of goods and services). Historical experience – as reviewed in the last two chapters – has shown that the direction of causation is from money to asset prices and expenditure, not the other way round. The Kaldorian critique and the analysis of the narrow-money school do not stand up. Another critique of the monetary approach needs to be discussed, however. Numerous statements can be found – at both the popular level and in the publications of professional economists – to the effect that 'credit' is relevant to the determination of both asset prices and national expenditure. Indeed, some authors put credit ahead of money. This chapter will argue that the elevation of credit *by itself* to a prominent role in national income determination is a mistake. On the other hand, it very much endorses the proposition that a particular type of credit, namely bank credit, is important to the business cycle. The significance of bank credit arises not from its independent influence on economic variables, but from the part it plays in money creation.

Currency and banking schools

Some of the trouble in understanding this subject stems from imprecision in the use of words. Disputes about the meaning of words were a recurrent element in the protracted battle of ideas between the currency and banking schools in England in the early nineteenth century. Even in the late nineteenth and early twentieth centuries terminology had not settled down. A common practice was to describe bank deposits as 'credit', because they arose from the extension of credit by the banks.[1] Nowadays, by contrast, the accepted convention is that bank deposits are 'money'. The uncertainties about words were accompanied, however, by deeper and more substantive disagreements. One of the earliest enthusiasts for a credit-based explanation of prices was John Stuart Mill in Chapter XII of Book 3 of *Principles of Political Economy*. In his words, 'It is obvious ... that prices do not depend on money, but on purchases.' Further,

> Credit which is used to purchase commodities, affects prices
> in the same manner as money. Money and credit are thus
> exactly on a par in their effect on prices; and whether we
> choose to class bank notes with the one or the other, is in
> this respect entirely immaterial.[2]

The difficulty with these remarks is that they are not placed in a convincing theoretical schema. Mill was acerbic in his references to 'the doctrine of the infancy of society and of political economy', stating that 'the quantity of money compared with that of commod-

1   David Laidler, *The Golden Age of the Quantity Theory* (Hemel Hempstead: Philip Allan, 1991), pp. 14–15.

2   V. W. Bladen and J. M. Robson (eds), *Principles of Political Economy*, vol. III of *Collected Works of John Stuart Mill* (London and Toronto: Routledge & Kegan Paul and University of Toronto Press, 1965, originally published 1848).

ities determines general prices'. But the truth is that this doctrine, far from being abandoned at the 'infancy of political economy', has been rigorously developed – at the level of individual agents and for all individuals in the aggregate, and in both partial and general equilibrium models – since Mill's day. As set out in Chapter 1 (for the markets in goods and services) and in Chapter 2 (for assets), one of the triumphs of monetary analysis is to reconcile the equilibrium of individual money-holding agents with equilibrium between the demand for and supply of money in the economy as a whole. No similar exercise has been carried out with credit-based theories.

Indeed, attempts to develop credit-based theories for the economy as a whole face a serious, perhaps insurmountable, conceptual problem. Mill is right that in any particular transaction prices 'do not depend on money, but on purchases', and that an isolated purchase can be financed by credit. But the question has to be asked, 'Where does the credit come from?' Assuming that expenditure is not financed from money or asset holdings, any one agent can spend above income because it has received credit, but the agent extending credit has to offset this by spending beneath income. A person or a company can receive credit from or extend credit to another person or company, but a society cannot – in net terms – receive credit from or extend credit to itself. If international complications are ignored, the sum of net credit in any economy in any period is zero. No economist has developed a theory in which credit *by itself* determines the aggregate price level, because any such theory would be logically impossible. A purchase financed by credit can influence prices in an isolated transaction; purchases financed by credit cannot determine the overall price level because all agents taken together cannot be net recipients of credit.

Modern proponents of credit

But this difficulty – so compelling at the aggregate level – has not deterred economists from assembling sentences and paragraphs ('quasi-theories') in which credit is given a starring role. In a chapter on 'A general theory of reform' in his 1973 book on *Economics and the Public Purpose*, Galbraith wanted 'to reduce ... for all time the use of monetary policy'. He saw monetary policy as equivalent to 'reducing or increasing ... the amount of money available for borrowing', and claimed it suffered from intrinsic uncertainty about its effects. In his words, 'No one knows what the response to a greater or less availability of funds for borrowing will be or when that response will occur, for the reason that the factors that govern such response are never the same from one time to the next.' He also opposed – apparently at any time and in any economy – interest rates increases to limit credit 'and therewith the volume of spending from borrowed funds and therewith, also, for that matter the supply of money'.[3]

Much has gone wrong here. To repeat, at the aggregate level, the concept of 'the amount of money available for borrowing' is vacuous. In net terms the amount of credit is, always and everywhere, precisely nil. Of course, a sum can be borrowed and lent, recorded in a written IOU and registered in a balance sheet. Further, it may survive from period to period, adding to the gross totals of credit and debt outstanding. Galbraith is simply wrong, however, to equate 'the volume of spending from borrowed funds' with 'the money supply', unless he defines the phrase 'the money supply' in an idiosyncratic way. True enough, when a bank extends new credit, it normally increases its assets and its deposit

3   John Kenneth Galbraith, *Economics and the Public Purpose* (Boston, MA: Houghton Mifflin, 1973), pp. 308–9.

liabilities, and the deposit liabilities are money. But borrowing and lending are also performed between non-bank agents, and in such cases no new money is created. When a company extends credit to a customer (helping it 'to spend from borrowed funds'), the level of trade credit expands, but trade credit is not money. Similarly, when a financial institution purchases a bond newly issued by a company (also helping it 'to spend from borrowed funds'), the level of credit in the bond market expands, but corporate bonds are not money. Vast amounts of lending and borrowing, of credit extension and registration, can take place, without affecting the quantity of money.

Despite the conceptual insecurity of credit-based theories of the price level, Galbraith has had several successors. One of the most influential has been Benjamin Friedman, professor of economics at Harvard University, who in the 1980s published a number of papers examining the facts of the relationships between money, credit and national income in the USA in the twentieth century. He did not propose an elaborate large-scale econometric model, but confined the analysis to bi-variate annual relationships between nominal money and nominal GDP, real money and nominal GDP, credit and real GDP, and so on. 'Credit' was measured by domestic non-financial credit (i.e. the stock of credit extended to the non-financial sectors of the US economy, including the public sector and the non-financial private sector). He corroborated the findings of, for example, Milton Friedman and Schwartz that '[m]oney growth consistently helps explain both nominal and real economic growth'. But there was a sting in the tail. In addition to money helping in the explanation of incomes and output, 'nominal and real income growth typically helps explain money growth' and – according to certain rigorous statistical techniques – that makes the pattern of causation ambiguous. By contrast, 'credit growth helps to explain nominal income, but not *vice versa*, in the second half of the post-war period' and '[f]or the post-war period as a whole, credit growth again helps to explain nominal income growth, while the reverse effect is only marginally significant'.[4] (The quotations are from a paper published in 1986. Benjamin Friedman's post-war period was from 1947 to 1982, and it was split into two sub-periods, 1947–65 and 1966–82.)

Benjamin Friedman's work appears unsettling for the supporters of the monetary theory of national income determination. Its point is not that the monetary approach is wrong, but that it may not be the only or even the most persuasive way of describing the real world. Benjamin Friedman's results are unsatisfactory in a crucial respect, however: they are measurement without theory. To be more specific, they are highly aggregative, and do not acknowledge the wide variety of agents and motives involved in the financial transactions that lead to the growth of 'domestic non-financial credit'. When an attempt is made to link the agents and motives in particular credit transactions to such variables as nominal GDP, the implausibility of a credit-based theory becomes clear. Two types of credit were particularly important in the post-war period, credit to the government (i.e. the budget deficits that led to the growth of the public debt) and mortgage credit to individuals, predominantly to purchase houses. Careful reflection shows that there is unlikely to be a robust

---

4   Benjamin M. Friedman, 'Money, credit and interest rates in the business cycle',
     in Robert J. Gordon (ed.), *The American Business Cycle: Continuity and Change*
     (Chicago and London: University of Chicago Press, 1986), pp. 395–458. The quo-
     tations are from pp. 421–2.

relationship between such credit and the expenditure components of GDP, unless the monetisation of debt via the banking system is the heart of the story.

Public debt may be taken first. Why should there be a relationship between it and either public or private expenditure? The Galbraithian quasi-theory might be invoked, on the grounds that a budget deficit enables the government 'to spend from borrowed funds'. But in most societies the bulk of government expenditure is financed from taxation and the ratio of tax to national income varies substantially over time. Inspection of the data shows that government expenditure is *not* clearly related to either the level or the rate of change of public debt. Moreover, the same net-credit-is-always-nil objection applies as before. To the extent that the government can spend more because it is borrowing, other agents (i.e. in the private sector) have to spend less because they are lending. To escape from this box, public debt has to alter the behaviour of private agents through portfolio effects. If Benjamin Friedman's analysis were on the right lines, private-sector expenditure ought somehow to be a positive function of public debt. But – unless the public debt is monetised – there is neither a convincing theory nor a substantial body of evidence to argue for this proposition. Indeed, a salient feature of historical experience is that the ratios of public debt to GDP can vary enormously over time, taking values between nil and over 200 per cent.

What about mortgage credit? The difficulty here is even more basic. An obtrusive fact about housing markets all over the world is that the purpose of most mortgages is to acquire an existing house (this is certainly the case in the USA). In other words, when it extends a mortgage, a bank is likely to be lending to an individual to buy a house that has already been built (i.e. that formed part of *past* output). But how then can the loan contribute to extra expenditure on goods and services or – in other words – to the expenditure that figures in the textbook circular flow of *current* output and expenditure? The mortgage money is absorbed by the purchase price of the house; the borrower cannot 'spend from borrowed money' (to use Galbraith's phrase again), in the sense of spending on consumption and thereby adding to national expenditure.[5] Indeed, to the extent that credit is extended in order to purchase assets, there is no immediate effect on national expenditure, output and income whatsoever. Instead credit of this kind facilitates transactions in assets. Such transactions may figure in Keynes's financial circulation, and – as we saw in Chapter 2 – the financial and industrial circulations are interrelated. But loans to purchase *existing* assets do not have any initial impact on the circular flow of income and expenditure where, according to the elementary textbooks, national income is determined.[6]

In fact, because most lenders require collateral to give them comfort that a loan will be repaid, the great bulk of credit to

5 It is true that once the vendor has received the proceeds of the mortgage loan he or she may decide to consume part of them. Another response, however, is to reinvest in another asset, including possibly a financial asset. The central point in the text – that mortgage lending has no direct or certain effect on the circular flow of income and expenditure – is correct, despite the wide variety of eventual destinations of mortgage funds. (For further discussion, see Congdon and Turnbull, 'Introducing the concept of "mortgage equity withdrawal"', in Tim Congdon, *Reflections on Monetarism*, pp. 274–87, as well as several recent papers by Bank staff in the Bank of England's *Quarterly Bulletin*.)

6 This point may cause puzzlement. In macroeconomic jargon, national expenditure consists of consumption and investment, where investment represents the acquisition of *newly created* capital assets, i.e. extra capital goods that form part of the current period's output and require resources of labour, capital and so on to be produced. Turnover in *existing* capital assets can be enormous relative to investment in this sense, but because the assets have already been made purchases are not a contribution to current output and sales are not a deduction from it.

the private sector is to purchase existing assets of some kind. While this feature of real-world credit is particularly obvious with mortgage lending to individuals, it is also true of lending to companies and financial institutions. Companies borrow from banks typically to make an investment in an existing asset (the purchase of another company, the acquisition of a building or piece of land, additions to inventories of raw materials or finished goods) and, in almost every case, the bank checks that it has adequate collateral. Occasionally companies borrow from capital markets with a vague explanation on the lines of 'for general corporate purposes', but stock market analysts distrust companies that do this too often. It may be a sign that they are borrowing in order to cover negative cash flow, but such Galbraithian 'spending from borrowed funds' cannot be recurrent because the company will eventually go bust.

In short, most loans to the private sector are to finance the acquisition of *existing* assets; they have no first-round effect on national expenditure and income. The Galbraithian quasi-theory of 'extra spending from borrowed funds', and Benjamin Friedman's attempts to promote a credit-based theory of national income determination from long runs of empirical data, break down when confronted with well-known facts of real-world economies. Although the Benjamin Friedman findings are thought-provoking, they need to be backed up by an explicit theory of the relationship between credit and national income. Without such a theory, his critique of the monetary approach is not persuasive.[7]

---

7   In fact, the empirical regularity behind Benjamin Friedman's findings – that in the USA non-financial debt and nominal GDP had grown at similar annual rates between 1947 and 1982 – broke down in the 1980s. From 1982 to 1987 non-financial debt increased at an annual compound rate of 13.4 per cent, whereas nominal GDP increased at an annual compound rate of 7.8 per cent.

Clearly, the observation that in the real world credit is directed, overwhelmingly, to the purchase of assets is awkward for those credit-based theories in which credit is supposed to affect purchases of goods and services (and so national income). The prominence of credit in asset acquisition, however, has generated another quasi-theory, that the amount of 'borrowing' has a bearing on the level of asset prices. Numerous loosely theoretical remarks on these lines are found in the financial press and popular business books, but sometimes they migrate to more serious works. One example is a recent volume on *Bubbles and How to Survive Them* by the financial economist John Calverley. In it he proposes – if in a fairly casual way – a theory in which the quantity and terms of mortgage lending affect the level of house prices.

After pointing out the contrasting behaviour of household debt in leading industrial nations in the five years to 2003 (with debt soaring in the USA, the UK and Australia, where house prices were increasing, but debt static in Japan and Germany, where house prices were flat), he suggested that 'the bulk of the increase in debt can only be explained in relation to home prices'.[8] His view is that well-capitalised banks may be tempted to relax their lending standards and to increase the multiple of income they lend to mortgagors. As a result, the level of house prices varies according to the lending practices of the banks. '[W]hen mortgages are agreed based on the appraised value of a house, while the value of housing is pushed higher by the easy availability of mortgages, there is a serious risk that house prices can reach extreme levels.' More generally, asset price 'bubbles normally do

---

8   John P. Calverley, *Bubbles and How to Survive Them* (London and Boston. MA:
     Nicholas Brealey Publishing, 2004), p. 107.

not develop without significant lending being involved, usually by banks'.[9]

Once again, the trouble with this hypothesis is that it is not grounded in a rigorous theory. Of course, if a particular home-buyer is able to borrow five times income rather than three times, he or she can pay more for a house. Certain individuals may be so financially inept that once the mortgage is available they pay up for the house, regardless of the wider economic picture. But most people are not like this. They make a judgement also about the appropriateness of the price of a particular house relative to the prices of numerous other similar houses, while wealth-holders in general are constantly comparing the price level of houses with that of other assets. Is Calverley claiming that mortgage borrowing affects both house prices and all asset prices, or only house prices? And what is the mechanism at work? Does the change in mortgage lending determine the level or the change in the value of the housing stock? Or is it the stock of mortgage lending which determines these variables? What are the testable hypotheses of the theory (or quasi-theory) under consideration?

These questions may seem pedantic, but they suggest a way of confronting the lending-determines-asset-prices quasi-theory with an overwhelming counter-argument. Suppose that banks had no loan assets (i.e. there was no bank credit and, indeed, no mortgage credit), but that the money supply took a positive value because banks held government bonds and cash. Would the value

---

9   Ibid. The quotations are from pp. 110 and 161. The lending-determines-asset-prices quasi-theory is also found in Derek Scott's study of macroeconomic policy in the 1990s, *Off Whitehall* (London: I. B. Tauris, 2004). See p. 88, where it is said that 'excessive optimism will lead to unwise borrowing', which 'will lead to an asset price boom (particularly equities and housing)'. Such statements have become legion.

of the housing stock collapse to nothing because of the absence of mortgage credit? Merely to put the question is to identify a decisive flaw in the lending-determines-asset-prices theory. Of course houses would have value in an economy without mortgage credit. The correct theory must start from a proposition in which money is a key operative term. More precisely, agents are in equilibrium only when they are satisfied with the valuations of all assets (houses, equities, land, antiques) and the relative amounts of money and non-money assets in their portfolios.

It is obvious that a society can be entirely without mortgage credit and housing finance, and yet houses will have a positive value. By extension, a society can have a stock of mortgage credit *and a freeze on all new mortgage credit*, and yet still experience rapid house price increases because the quantity of money is rising too quickly. The monetary expansion may be due to heavy government borrowing from the banking system and so have nothing whatever to do with mortgage credit. But – because every agent has a finite demand for real money balances, because goods can be sold for assets and assets for goods, and because of the pervasiveness of arbitrage between assets (as explained in Chapter 2) – high money supply growth is associated with high house price inflation. It is money, not credit, which is relevant to determining the general level of asset prices.[10]

Another way of seeing this point is to recall one message of Chapter 3. It was shown there that the portfolio behaviour of large financial institutions, such as pension funds and life assurance

---

10   When Calverley comes to consider asset busts and the risk that the economy may fall into a 'liquidity trap', his discussion is about the adequacy of money balances, not about bank borrowing or credit. See Calverley, *Bubbles*, pp. 177–9. Why are asset prices explained by money in a bust, but by credit in a boom?

companies, had a powerful bearing on asset price movements in the UK in the closing decades of the twentieth century. But most of these institutions either never borrowed or did so only for temporary and special reasons (such as to cover a very short-term timing mismatch in security transactions or to support an investment in commercial property). By contrast, over the medium term the growth rate of these institutions' money holdings had a clear relationship with the growth rate of their total assets. Money, not borrowing or credit, was what mattered in large institutions' portfolio decisions.

The common belief in the macroeconomic importance of credit stems from a confusion. In recent decades a characteristic feature of most banking systems is that the growth of liabilities (dominated by deposits, i.e. by money) has been highly correlated with the growth of bank credit, where 'bank credit' is to be understood as bank lending to the private sector. As national income and asset prices are correlated with money, it has been tempting to say also that national income and asset prices are correlated with bank credit. Some economists go farther. Since it is undoubtedly true that new bank loans usually create new bank deposits, they accord credit the primary role in the process. Their mistake is twofold.

First, they need to check whether non-bank credit has the same power to alter macroeconomic outcomes as bank credit. As it happens, abundant data on various types of non-bank credit (such as trade credit and new bond issues) are compiled by official statistical agencies in most countries. Tests need to be carried out to see whether such non-bank credit variables have a clear relationship with other macroeconomic numbers. As far as the author is aware, no economist has proposed that nominal national income is a function of trade credit or new bond issuance, and no worthwhile econometric results hint at the validity of such propositions. It follows that credit matters to macroeconomic outcomes only when it is extended by banks and is accompanied by the creation of money.

Second, banks can expand in two ways: by making new loans or by buying existing securities.[11] When they buy existing securities, they are not extending new credit. Nevertheless, their liabilities – usually their deposit liabilities (i.e. money) – increase because they must give IOUs to the sellers of the securities. Conversely, banks can shrink their balance sheets by selling securities. It follows that money can expand or contract even when bank credit is unchanged. In some periods the influence of the banks' securities transactions on changes in the quantity of money has been greater than the influence of their credit activities. If credit were the key macroeconomic variable, these periods ought to have seen a breakdown in the standard relationships between money and the economy. Is that what has been observed in practice?

Strictly speaking, a large-scale empirical exercise – dealing with many countries in many periods – is needed to answer this question. The discussion here has to be rather truncated and will concentrate on British experience. As it happens, the post-war decades have seen a marked trend for banks to shed securities and to build up loan portfolios. In the late 1940s UK banks' assets were dominated by holdings of government bonds; nowadays such holdings are a tiny proportion of total assets. Indeed, in the last

---

11   This is a simplification, as liabilities also expand when banks take cash deposits from the public and when they book profits by charging interest. Note also that purchases of securities add to the quantity of money only when the purchases are from private-sector non-banks.

30 years the growth rates of bank credit to the private sector and the growth rates of deposits in the M4 money definition have been closely correlated. This period is therefore unsuitable for testing the theory that it is the quantity of money, not the type of assets that banks hold, which is relevant to macroeconomic outcomes.

A better candidate is provided by the period from 1921 to 1945, covering both the inter-war period and World War II. In the 1920s and 1930s UK banks tried to keep their assets balanced between 'advances' (i.e. bank loans to the private sector) and 'investments', which were predominantly short-dated and medium-dated government securities.[12] They also held significant amounts of Treasury bills and commercial bills (so-called 'liquid assets'), which could be easily bought and sold in an organised market, and were often purchased with cash by the Bank of England. Figures 11 and 12 show the changing composition of London clearing banks' assets between 1921 and 1945.[13] The 1920s saw a rise in the share of advances in total assets, from 40.6 per cent in 1921 to 49.3 per cent in 1929, as the banks shed some of the government securities they had acquired in World War I. The figure fell sharply to 34.6 per cent in 1935, partly because the banks were keen to buy safe government securities in the deflationary circumstances of the time. During World War II the banks were prevented from expanding their advances to the private sector because military expenditure had priority. They were obliged instead to lend to the government at an artificially low interest rate. (The banks accumulated the resulting claims on the government as 'Treasury

12 Short-dated securities were defined as those having a residual maturity of under five years and medium-dated securities as those having a residual maturity of between five and fifteen years.

13 At these dates the London clearing banks dominated the English banking scene and the English banking industry dominated that in the UK as a whole.

Figure 11 **Composition of UK banks' assets, levels, 1921–45**
£m

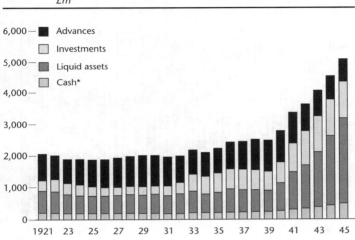

*'Cash' includes deposit at Bank of England.
Source: Edward Nevin and E. W. Davis, *The London Clearing Banks* (London: Elek Books, 1970),
pp. 298–9

Deposit Receipts', which were deemed to be liquid assets.) By 1945 advances were under 15 per cent of the London clearing banks' total assets.

So the 1921–45 period saw large changes in the relative importance of different bank assets, with credit to the private sector often moving inversely with other bank assets and having no clear correlation with the growth of the money supply. Which of the two variables – the money supply or bank lending to the private sector – mattered to national income determination? The answer is provided by Figures 13 and 14. Figure 13 shows

Figure 12 **Composition of UK banks' assets, 1921–45**
% of assets

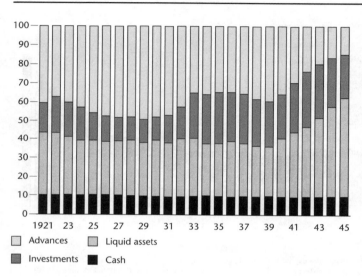

☐ Advances   ☐ Liquid assets

■ Investments   ■ Cash

*'Cash' includes deposit at Bank of England.
Source: Edward Nevin and E. W. Davis, *The London Clearing Banks* (London: Elek Books, 1970), pp. 298–9

that national income and the money supply were correlated, in accordance with traditional monetary theory. It is particularly striking that national income rose strongly (by almost 66 per cent) during World War II, when credit restrictions stopped lending to the private sector. Figure 14 plots the London clearing banks' advances against national income. No correlation of any kind holds between the two series.[14]

---

14   The author carried out regressions of gross national product at factor cost on two variables – the money supply (i.e. notes and coin in circulation with the public, and the London clearing banks' deposits) and the London clearing banks' ad-

Figure 13 **National income and money, 1921–45**
          £m

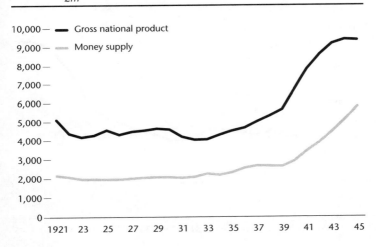

Source: Edward Nevin and E. W. Davis, *The London Clearing Banks* (London: Elek Books, 1970), pp. 290–2 and pp. 298–9

Economic theory is not immutable; it changes with fashion and in response to events. In the 1930s, 1940s and 1950s British monetary economists regarded 'the money supply' as the sum of notes and coin in circulation with the general public, and virtually all bank deposits held at UK banks.[15] Moreover, because loans to the private sector were only a proportion of banks'

vances – in the 1921–45 period. The r-squared on the equation with the money supply was 0.91, whereas on the equation with advances it was 0.01.

15   These years were the heyday of Keynes's influence on UK economics. Keynes stated his view on the appropriate definition of money in a footnote to Chapter 13 of *The General Theory*, and specifically stated that it was often convenient to include time deposits in 'the quantity of money'. See also footnote 4 on page 90.

Figure 14 **National income and bank lending, 1921–45**
£m

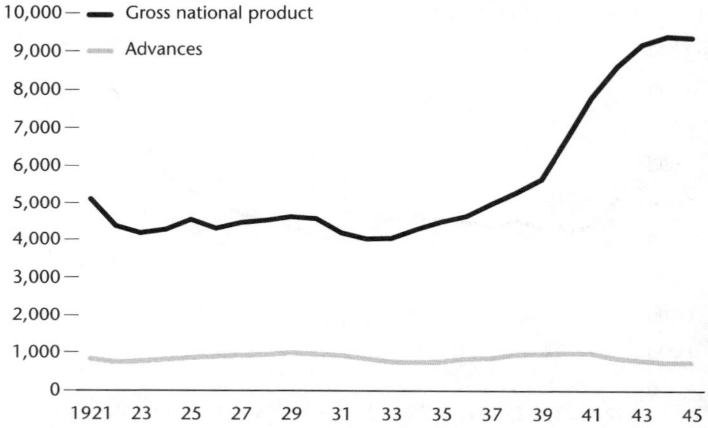

Source: Edward Nevin and E. W. Davis, *The London Clearing Banks* (London: Elek Books, 1970), pp. 290–2 and pp. 298–9

total assets, monetary policy was heavily involved with issues of debt management.[16] The phrase 'debt management' described the efforts of 'the authorities' (i.e. the Treasury and the Bank of England) to market government debt in ways that would support their wider objectives. Sometimes (as in the 1930s) these objectives would be to promote output and employment, while at other times (from 1945) they would be to preserve the fixed exchange

16 For the prominence of debt management in monetary policy in the 1950s, see both the Radcliffe Report itself (*Report on the Committee on the Working of the Monetary System* [London: HMSO, 1959]) and, for example, the chapter on monetary policy by Charles Kennedy, in G. D. N. Worswick and P. H. Ady (eds), *The British Economy in the Nineteen-Fifties* (Oxford: Clarendon Press, 1962), pp. 301–25.

rate between the pound and the dollar, and to restrain inflation. It was uncontroversial that, if commercial banks bought government debt, this would increase the amount of money in the economy and boost equilibrium national income. In contrast to the fashions of the 1990s, monetary policy was not equated with bank lending to the private sector and it was regarded as something more than the adjustment of short-term interest rates to keep output in line with trend. It is clear from the basic monetary facts of the era – in which changes in banks' claims on government were so fundamental to money supply developments – that the emphases of contemporary monetary economists in the 1930s and 1940s were sensible. They were right to neglect bank credit to the private sector, because such credit did not have a significant role in monetary management.[17]

The larger message from the experience of the inter-war period and World War II is the same as that from our earlier review of the credit-based quasi-theories of national income. These quasi-theories do not stand up either when confronted with serious theoretical probing or when tested against the facts of the real world. Over the last 30 or 40 years bank credit to the private sector and the money supply have had a close relationship in most industrial nations, which has misled some economists into believing that the valid relationship is between bank credit and nominal

---

17 See Harry G. Johnson, 'Clearing bank holdings of public debt, 1930–50', *London & Cambridge Economic Service Bulletin* (Cambridge: University of Cambridge Department of Applied Economics), November 1951 issue, pp. 1–8, particularly the chart on p. 8. The emphasis of British monetary economists on debt management continued even into the 1950s, when bank credit to the private sector was resurgent. The discussion of monetary policy in, for example, F. W. Paish's 'Inflation in the United Kingdom, 1948–57', *Economica*, May 1958, pp. 94–105, is largely about the relationship between, on the one hand, fiscal policy and debt management and, on the other, the amount of money in the economy.

national income, rather than between the money supply and nominal national income. It is essential that the statistical testing be conducted in periods – such as the 25 years to 1945 – when bank credit and the money supply moved in divergent ways. In such periods national income is related to the money supply, but not to bank credit. Credit *by itself* does not determine either national income or asset prices. The argument of traditional monetary theory – that the national income is in equilibrium only when the demand to hold money is equal to the money supply, and that in this sense the money supply determines national income – is correct. Credit-based analyses have never been presented with the same level of care and sophistication as the monetary theory of national income, and they have not been incorporated in rigorous discussions of portfolio selection (i.e. in discussions of asset price determination). They must be rejected as inadequate and unsatisfactory.

6 CONCLUSION: MONEY AND ASSET PRICES IN THE TRANSMISSION MECHANISM

Nowadays most accounts of the transmission mechanism of monetary policy give pride of place to the level of interest rates or even to only one interest rate (i.e. the central bank rediscount rate) as the economy's factotum. An alternative approach, building on the work of Irving Fisher, Patinkin and Friedman, sees expenditure decisions as motivated by individuals' attempts to bring actual money balances into line with the demand to hold them. Many introductory statements in this tradition focus on the effect that these attempts have initially on expenditure on goods and services, and eventually on the price level. They rely for their conclusions on two features of the adjustment process, the stability of the desired ratio of money balances to expenditure, and the distinction between the 'individual experiment' and the 'market experiment' in a closed circuit of payments where the quantity of money is kept constant. This paper has shown that the same sort of story can be told about asset markets, relying on the stability of financial institutions' desired ratio of money balances to asset totals and the invariance of the pool of institutional money balances as asset prices are changing. It follows that, when the quantity of money held by key players in asset markets rises or falls abruptly by a large amount, powerful forces are at work to increase or lower asset prices.

Of course, the notion of a closed circuit of payments – for

either goods and services or assets – is a simplification. In the real world, markets in goods and services are not separate from asset markets. If excess money leads to a rise in asset prices, almost certainly the rise in asset prices will influence expenditure on goods and services. As noted in Chapter 1, in his 1959 statement to the US Congress, Friedman compared the rounds of payments as agents seek to restore monetary equilibrium (i.e. the equivalence of the demand for and supply of money balances) to a game of musical chairs. In Chapter 3 of this monograph the venue for the game of musical chairs was the UK economy, including its asset markets. Moreover, because of the availability of sectoral money supply data in the UK since 1963, it has become possible to say more about the identity and behaviour of the main players in the game. Three types of player in the UK in the 40-year period under review were individuals as such, companies and financial institutions. Companies and financial institutions were particularly active in asset price determination. It has been shown that the corporate and financial sectors' money balances were consistently more volatile than personal-sector money, and the volatility in their money holdings was reflected in asset prices. The relevant quantity of money here has to be an all-inclusive or broad money measure, partly because, in modern circumstances, agents managing large portfolios do not have significant note holdings.

Very high growth rates of broad money were therefore responsible for the asset price exuberance in the upturn phase of both the Heath–Barber boom in the early 1970s and the Lawson boom in the late 1980s, and subsequent very sharp declines in broad money growth were responsible for the asset price busts that followed. It has been possible to give an account of events with only an occasional reference to interest rates. Changes to expenditure on goods and services, and decisions to buy and sell assets, could be inter-preted as responses to excess or deficient money holdings, not to the putative effect of an interest rate on investment or stock-building. In the same spirit as the 'monetary' view espoused by Friedman and Meiselman back in 1964, the adequacy of agents' money holdings impinged on a very broad 'range of assets' and affected a very wide range of 'associated expenditures'.

The phrase 'too much money chasing too few goods' has been used to characterise an economy suffering from inflationary pres-sures and it does indeed convey the essence of the transmission mechanism as seen by Fisher, Patinkin and Friedman. The phrase 'too much money chasing too few assets' was used during the Heath–Barber and Lawson booms in the UK, and again captures the spirit of the analytical sketch of asset price determination set out in this paper.[1] But in truth the right phrase is 'too much money chasing too few assets and too few goods', because asset markets are linked with markets in goods and services. One puzzle about the period discussed in the paper is that, while the Heath–Barber boom demonstrated the power of excess money growth to disturb asset markets and cause inflation, an essentially similar sequence of events was played out less than twenty years later with equally disastrous results. The puzzle is heightened by the apparent commitment of the Conservative government

---

[1]   The author used the phrase 'too much money chasing too few assets' in a news-paper article in *The Times* of 9 January 1986, in a reaction to the recent sharp upturn in money supply growth. But it was recognised that inflation was not im-minent. Immediately after the mention of money and assets, the comment was, 'But it is nonsense, while unemployment remains above three million, industry has abundant spare capacity and there is scope to increase output, to say that "too much money is chasing too few goods".' (The article, 'Why Lawson must repent', was reprinted as 'A forecast of a Lawson mini-boom', in Congdon, *Reflec-tions on Monetarism*, pp. 123–5.)

from 1979 to 'Thatcherite monetarism', including a medium-term financial strategy that was intended to outlaw excessive money supply growth. Just as 'monetarism' had developed in the 1970s by the import of largely American ideas, so the abandonment of the monetary element in that strategy reflected the influence of fashionable academic thinking on the other side of the Atlantic.[2] The decline in academic interest in 'the real-balance effect' (or whatever short phrase best denotes the genus of the transmission mechanism described in this paper) was basic to understanding official decisions and their often catastrophic consequences.

Admittedly, much of the account here has taken narrative form and suffers from the possible risk of being too selective with facts and figures. Two econometric exercises have been undertaken to address this weakness. In the first, changes in a composite asset price index are regressed on changes in non-personal broad money (i.e. the M4 balances held by the financial and company sectors combined), and in the second, changes in real private domestic demand are regressed on changes in real non-personal broad money. (Note that private domestic demand is the correct measure of demand for the purpose. Government spending must be excluded, because government spending is not sensitive to money holdings; exports must be excluded, because they reflect demand conditions elsewhere in the world.) The results – which are reported in the annex to this chapter – suggest that non-personal money holdings did have a significant effect on both

---

2   Minford attributes his own thinking on money – particularly his view that bank credit, bank deposits and the banking system are irrelevant to macroeconomic outcomes – to an American economist, Eugene Fama, and especially to two papers written by Fama in 1980 and 1983. See Minford, *Supply Side Revolution*, p. 73, and Minford, *Markets not Stakes*, p. 103.

asset prices and expenditure.[3] In short, the UK's boom–bust cycles in the closing four decades of the twentieth century reflected extreme fluctuations in money supply growth. Excess money was accompanied by asset price buoyancy, and provoked both above-trend growth in demand and exchange rate weakness. The eventual result was higher inflation. Similarly, deficient money was associated with asset price declines and slowdowns (or even contractions) in demand.

As shown by the review of US and Japanese experience at very different stages of the twentieth century in Chapter 4, the same sort of analytical framework can be readily applied to other nations at other times. In our discussion of the asset price oscillations that accompanied the Great Depression in the USA and preceded the Japanese malaise in the late 1990s, it has been essential to refer to an all-inclusive (or 'broad') measure of money. Several leading economists believe that narrow money measures are more useful and reliable in interpreting the behaviour of demand than broad money measures, with some even seeing a connection between the monetary base alone and macroeconomic conditions.[4] But in advanced industrial nations significant wealth-holders do not even consider notes and coin when reviewing

---

3   According to one analyst highly critical of the role of the money supply as policy guides, the results of his work showed that 'money holdings of OFIs might be the best leading indicator of money income of all the monetary variables', although qualifying this by noting that in Q2 1990 his equation over-predicted the OFIs' money holdings. He appeared not to entertain the possibility that the under-prediction relative to the equation indicated that the OFIs were short of money balances, and that this might affect future asset values and the economy (Garry Young, *The influence of financial intermediaries on the behaviour of the UK economy* [London: National Institute of Economic and Social Research, Occasional Papers no. 50, 1996], p. 97).

4   To be specific, Minford and McCallum favour the monetary base as a measure of monetary conditions, and Meltzer favours M1.

portfolios and taking major investment decisions. Nowadays all meaningful transactions in assets are conducted, and have long been conducted, by means of payment instructions against bank deposits. In practice, even time deposits can be easily mobilised by a phone call to one's bank manager. The claim that companies, financial institutions and wealthy individuals balance monetary base assets against non-monetary assets, and that they ignore bank deposits, is preposterous. The truth is instead that agents in control of large asset pools are hardly aware of their note and coin holdings, if indeed they have any at all. What matters to them in their portfolio decisions is their overall liquidity (i.e. the assets that can be moved quickly and at little cost, to effect purchases of less liquid higher-return assets). Moreover, bank deposits – and usually time deposits – are much the largest component of such liquidity totals. Keynes, in both his two classics, *The Treatise on Money* and *The General Theory of Employment, Interest and Money*, and Friedman and Schwartz, in their *Monetary History of the United States*, favoured money measures that included *all* bank deposits (meaning demand *and* time deposits), although in some circumstances they saw the virtues of a yet wider measure embracing other liquid assets. This support for broad money measures can be interpreted as part and parcel of a wider vision of how a modern economy works. In that vision money affects business activity largely through its effects on wealth portfolios and asset values.

The behaviour of the quantity of money, on the broad definitions, was fundamental to understanding the UK economy's changing cyclical fortunes over the 40-year period examined in this study, the stock market crash and the associated macroeconomic trauma in the USA between 1929 and 1933, and the stock market boom and bust in Japan in the late 1980s and early 1990s.[5] The behaviour of the quantity of money, on the broad definitions, will remain fundamental to understanding the behaviour of market economies in future.

Annexe

This paper has argued that the behaviour of the quantity of

---

5   An anonymous referee has wondered whether the asset price excesses seen in economic history (the tulip mania, the South Sea bubble, etc.) are also to be explained in money supply terms. Of course, this is an enormous question, related to the much debated topic of the relative importance of real and monetary forces in business cycle fluctuations. The difficulty with identifying a link between the money supply (understood as a concept with a significant component in the form of bank deposits) and asset prices before the thirteenth and fourteenth centuries is that the banking system was embryonic. Of course, in the absence of banks, the money stock was dominated by the precious metals, not by bank deposits. Later the problem changed. Even when banks started to become common, meaningful data from which estimates of the money supply could be prepared were rare. Such data were first published in most countries only in the late nineteenth century. Even in the late medieval period, however, it is possible to find several historical episodes in which the collapse of proto-banks was associated with asset price weakness and depressed output. See, for example, ch. I, 'The Great Crash of 1343–46', in Carlo M. Cipolla, *The Monetary Policy of Fourteenth-Century Florence* (Berkeley: University of California Press, 1982), pp. 1–29. After describing the loss of bank deposits between 1343 and 1346, Cipolla noted (on pp. 13–14) that not only had the market in public debt plummeted, but '[m]ore telling was the collapse of real estate values ... [P]rices of real estate in the city fell by about 50 per cent, and in the country property fell by about a third, and still "no buyer was to be found"'. One of the great achievements of Irving Fisher's *The Purchasing Power of Money* (1911), as discussed in Chapter 1, was to assemble data on the quantity of money and the price level of goods and services in many countries and over several long periods. Its ambition was remarkable, including a Figure 10 in Chapter XI (on 'Statistical verification: general historical review') on prices going back to AD 800! 'According to the diagram prices are now about five times as high as in the period between 1200 and 1500 AD' (p. 234). But Fisher could not put together data on asset price movements as well, not least because organised asset markets are a relatively recent innovation.

money, broadly defined, was fundamental in explaining cyclical fluctuations in the UK economy in the closing four decades of the twentieth century. It has focused, in particular, on the money balances of financial institutions and companies, because of their special relevance to asset price determination.

Figure 4 (see p. 60) showed the relationship between annual changes in the sum of non-household M4 balances, and annual changes in a composite price index, using quarterly data. The composite price index was estimated with three components, the FT Industrial Ordinary Index (for share prices), the Nationwide house price index (for house prices) and the Hillier-Parker index of commercial property values (for commercial property). The weights were 40 per cent for both share prices and house prices, and 20 per cent for commercial property prices. The FT Industrial Ordinary Index is available back to 1935 and the Nationwide house price index to 1954. The commercial property component in the 1960s was less satisfactory as the Hillier-Parker index started in 1972. For the early years it was constructed by assuming that it behaved in the same way as an equally weighted combination of share and house prices.[6] An equation regressing the asset price index on non-household money was estimated and is reported below.

Change in composite price index % = 2.97 + 0.42
(Change in non-household money) %

---

6   Mr Richard Wild of the Office for National Statistics helped in the preparation of the composite asset price index.

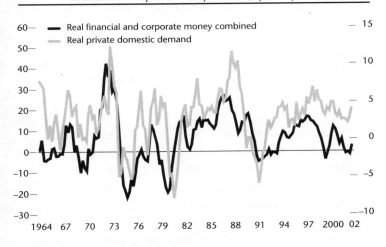

Figure 15 **Money and demand in the UK, 1964–2002**
Annual % changes in real private domestic demand and sum of real financial and corporate money balances, quarterly data

Source: National Statistics website and author's calculations

r squared	0.25
Standard error of equation	8.09
Standard error for intercept term	1.02
Standard error of regression coefficient	0.06
t statistic for intercept term	2.92
t statistic for regression coefficient	7.24

Figure 15 shows the relationship between annual changes in the sum of M4 balances held by financial institutions and companies in real terms (where the GDP deflator was used to make the adjustment from nominal to real terms), and annual changes in private domestic demand, also in real terms, and (as with Figure 4) using quarterly data. An equation relating the change in real demand to the change in real non-household money was estimated and is reported below.

Change in real private domestic demand (%) = 1.74 + 0.174
(Change in non-household money, in real terms) %

r squared	0.32
Standard error of equation	2.99
Standard error for intercept term	0.27
Standard error of regression coefficient	0.02
t statistic for intercept term	6.39
t statistic for regression coefficient	8.43

Note, from the regression coefficients in the two equations, that fluctuations in non-household M4 had greater amplitude than those in asset prices, and that asset prices were more volatile than real private domestic demand. It has been necessary – in Figure 15 – to have two axes on different scales to capture this difference in volatility.

Appendix: **THE REAL BALANCE EFFECT**

This claim that the real balance effect is at the heart of the transmission mechanism from money to the real economy is controversial. Patinkin regarded the real balance effect as a kind of wealth effect. It was pointed out that, as the banking system's assets and liabilities must be equal, that part of the quantity of money represented by banks' deposit liabilities (so-called 'inside money', from a distinction proposed by Gurley and Shaw in their 1960 *Theory of Finance*) could not represent a nation's net wealth. A logical implication was that the real balance effect related only to 'outside money', often taken to be equivalent to monetary base assets issued by the central bank. It was then shown that, since the monetary base is modest compared with other elements in a nation's wealth, the real balance effect is small and cannot have a powerful influence on macroeconomic outcomes.[1]

The emphasis in macroeconomic theory moved away from the real balance effect towards 'the Keynes effect', to be understood as the effect of changes in the quantity of money on interest rates and so on investment. An argument can be made, however, that the only concept of money relevant to the real balance effect is an all-inclusive measure, since agents can eliminate excesses or deficiencies of smaller, less-than-inclusive measures by transfers

---

1   See, in particular, Thomas Mayer, 'The empirical significance of the real balance effect', *Quarterly Journal of Economics* (vol. 73, no. 2 , 1959), pp. 275–91.

between money balances (i.e. they can switch between sight and time deposits, or between notes and sight deposits). Such 'money transfers' plainly have no effect on aggregate demand or asset dispositions. By implication, if the real balance effect is indeed the *sine qua non* of monetary theory, it must relate to inside money and cannot be exclusively a wealth effect.[2]

Laidler has also used the phrase 'the real balance effect' to mean something more than just a wealth effect and claimed that, in the US economy for the years 1954–78, 'the adjustment of real balances towards the desired long-run values has a pervasive and systematic influence on the macroeconomy'.[3]

Note also that the claim that outside money, i.e. the central bank's liabilities, constitutes net wealth to the private sector of the economy is debatable. It would obviously be invalid if the central bank's assets were all claims on the private sector. But even if government securities were all of the central bank's assets and – in accordance with Barro's doctrine of Ricardian equivalence – government debt were judged not to be net wealth to the private sector, then

a) outside money also cannot be net wealth to the private sector; and
b) the private sector's net wealth cannot be increased when the central bank expands its balance sheet.

Yet virtually all macroeconomists accept that something

---

2   See Tim Congdon, 'Broad money vs. narrow money', *The Review of Policy Issues* (Sheffield: Policy Research Centre, 1995), vol. 1, no. 5, pp. 13–27, for further discussion.

3   David Laidler, *Money and Macroeconomics* (Cheltenham: Edward Elgar, 1997), p. 172.

important happens when the central bank shifts the position of the supply curve of the monetary base and changes short-term interest rates. If this effect is not a net wealth effect, how does it change anything and why does it matter? And, if it matters so much even though it is not a wealth effect, why is it that changes in inside money do not matter at all?

ABOUT THE IEA

The Institute is a research and educational charity (No. CC 235 351), limited by guarantee. Its mission is to improve understanding of the fundamental institutions of a free society with particular reference to the role of markets in solving economic and social problems.

The IEA achieves its mission by:

- a high-quality publishing programme
- conferences, seminars, lectures and other events
- outreach to school and college students
- brokering media introductions and appearances

The IEA, which was established in 1955 by the late Sir Antony Fisher, is an educational charity, not a political organisation. It is independent of any political party or group and does not carry on activities intended to affect support for any political party or candidate in any election or referendum, or at any other time. It is financed by sales of publications, conference fees and voluntary donations.

In addition to its main series of publications the IEA also publishes a quarterly journal, *Economic Affairs*.

The IEA is aided in its work by a distinguished international Academic Advisory Council and an eminent panel of Honorary Fellows. Together with other academics, they review prospective IEA publications, their comments being passed on anonymously to authors. All IEA papers are therefore subject to the same rigorous independent refereeing process as used by leading academic journals.

IEA publications enjoy widespread classroom use and course adoptions in schools and universities. They are also sold throughout the world and often translated/reprinted.

Since 1974 the IEA has helped to create a world-wide network of 100 similar institutions in over 70 countries. They are all independent but share the IEA's mission.

Views expressed in the IEA's publications are those of the authors, not those of the Institute (which has no corporate view), its Managing Trustees, Academic Advisory Council members or senior staff.

Members of the Institute's Academic Advisory Council, Honorary Fellows, Trustees and Staff are listed on the following page.

The Institute gratefully acknowledges financial support for its publications programme and other work from a generous benefaction by the late Alec and Beryl Warren.

143

Other papers recently published by the IEA include:

WHO, What and Why?

Transnational Government, Legitimacy and the World Health Organization
Roger Scruton
Occasional Paper 113; ISBN 0 255 36487 3
£8.00

The World Turned Rightside Up

A New Trading Agenda for the Age of Globalisation
John C. Hulsman
Occasional Paper 114; ISBN 0 255 36495 4
£8.00

The Representation of Business in English Literature

Introduced and edited by Arthur Pollard
Readings 53; ISBN 0 255 36491 1
£12.00

Anti-Liberalism 2000

The Rise of New Millennium Collectivism
David Henderson
Occasional Paper 115; ISBN 0 255 36497 0
£7.50

Capitalism, Morality and Markets

Brian Griffiths, Robert A. Sirico, Norman Barry & Frank Field
Readings 54; ISBN 0 255 36496 2
£7.50

A Conversation with Harris and Seldon

Ralph Harris & Arthur Seldon
Occasional Paper 116; ISBN 0 255 36498 9
£7.50

Malaria and the DDT Story

Richard Tren & Roger Bate
Occasional Paper 117; ISBN 0 255 36499 7
£10.00

A Plea to Economists Who Favour Liberty: Assist the Everyman

Daniel B. Klein
Occasional Paper 118; ISBN 0 255 36501 2
£10.00

The Changing Fortunes of Economic Liberalism

Yesterday, Today and Tomorrow
David Henderson
Occasional Paper 105 (new edition); ISBN 0 255 36520 9
£12.50

The Global Education Industry

Lessons from Private Education in Developing Countries
James Tooley
Hobart Paper 141 (new edition); ISBN 0 255 36503 9
£12.50

Saving Our Streams

*The Role of the Anglers' Conservation Association in
Protecting English and Welsh Rivers*
Roger Bate
Research Monograph 53; ISBN 0 255 36494 6
£10.00

Better Off Out?

The Benefits or Costs of EU Membership
Brian Hindley & Martin Howe
Occasional Paper 99 (new edition); ISBN 0 255 36502 0
£10.00

Buckingham at 25

Freeing the Universities from State Control
Edited by James Tooley
Readings 55; ISBN 0 255 36512 8
£15.00

Lectures on Regulatory and Competition Policy
Irwin M. Stelzer
Occasional Paper 120; ISBN 0 255 36511 X
£12.50

Misguided Virtue
False Notions of Corporate Social Responsibility
David Henderson
Hobart Paper 142; ISBN 0 255 36510 1
£12.50

HIV and Aids in Schools
The Political Economy of Pressure Groups and Miseducation
Barrie Craven, Pauline Dixon, Gordon Stewart & James Tooley
Occasional Paper 121; ISBN 0 255 36522 5
£10.00

The Road to Serfdom
The Reader's Digest *condensed version*
Friedrich A. Hayek
Occasional Paper 122; ISBN 0 255 36530 6
£7.50

Bastiat's *The Law*
Introduction by Norman Barry
Occasional Paper 123; ISBN 0 255 36509 8
£7.50

A Globalist Manifesto for Public Policy
Charles Calomiris
Occasional Paper 124; ISBN 0 255 36525 X
£7.50

Euthanasia for Death Duties
Putting Inheritance Tax Out of Its Misery
Barry Bracewell-Milnes
Research Monograph 54; ISBN 0 255 36513 6
£10.00

Liberating the Land
The Case for Private Land-use Planning
Mark Pennington
Hobart Paper 143; ISBN 0 255 36508 X
£10.00

IEA Yearbook of Government Performance 2002/2003
Edited by Peter Warburton
Yearbook 1; ISBN 0 255 36532 2
£15.00

Britain's Relative Economic Performance, 1870–1999
Nicholas Crafts
Research Monograph 55; ISBN 0 255 36524 1
£10.00

Should We Have Faith in Central Banks?
Otmar Issing
Occasional Paper 125; ISBN 0 255 36528 4
£7.50

The Dilemma of Democracy
Arthur Seldon
Hobart Paper 136 (reissue); ISBN 0 255 36536 5
£10.00

Capital Controls: a 'Cure' Worse Than the Problem?
Forrest Capie
Research Monograph 56; ISBN 0 255 36506 3
£10.00

The Poverty of 'Development Economics'
Deepak Lal
Hobart Paper 144 (reissue); ISBN 0 255 36519 5
£15.00

Should Britain Join the Euro?
The Chancellor's Five Tests Examined
Patrick Minford
Occasional Paper 126; ISBN 0 255 36527 6
£7.50

Post-Communist Transition: Some Lessons
Leszek Balcerowicz
Occasional Paper 127; ISBN 0 255 36533 0
£7.50

A Tribute to Peter Bauer
John Blundell et al.
Occasional Paper 128; ISBN 0 255 36531 4
£10.00

Employment Tribunals
Their Growth and the Case for Radical Reform
J. R. Shackleton
Hobart Paper 145; ISBN 0 255 36515 2
£10.00

Fifty Economic Fallacies Exposed

Geoffrey E. Wood

Occasional Paper 129; ISBN 0 255 36518 7

£12.50

A Market in Airport Slots

Keith Boyfield (editor), David Starkie, Tom Bass & Barry Humphreys

Readings 56; ISBN 0 255 36505 5

£10.00

Money, Inflation and the Constitutional Position of the Central Bank

Milton Friedman & Charles A. E. Goodhart

Readings 57; ISBN 0 255 36538 1

£10.00

railway.com

Parallels between the Early British Railways and the ICT Revolution

Robert C. B. Miller

Research Monograph 57; ISBN 0 255 36534 9

£12.50

The Regulation of Financial Markets

Edited by Philip Booth & David Currie

Readings 58; ISBN 0 255 36551 9

£12.50

Climate Alarmism Reconsidered

Robert L. Bradley Jr
Hobart Paper 146; ISBN 0 255 36541 1
£12.50

Government Failure: E. G. West on Education

Edited by James Tooley & James Stanfield
Occasional Paper 130; ISBN 0 255 36552 7
£12.50

Waging the War of Ideas

John Blundell
Second edition
Occasional Paper 131; ISBN 0 255 36547 0
£12.50

Corporate Governance: Accountability in the Marketplace

Elaine Sternberg
Second edition
Hobart Paper 147; ISBN 0 255 36542 X
£12.50

The Land Use Planning System

Evaluating Options for Reform
John Corkindale
Hobart Paper 148; ISBN 0 255 36550 0
£10.00

Economy and Virtue

Essays on the Theme of Markets and Morality
Edited by Dennis O'Keeffe
Readings 59; ISBN 0 255 36504 7
£12.50

Free Markets Under Siege

Cartels, Politics and Social Welfare
Richard A. Epstein
Occasional Paper 132; ISBN 0 255 36553 5
£10.00

Unshackling Accountants

D. R. Myddelton
Hobart Paper 149; ISBN 0 255 36559 4
£12.50

The Euro as Politics

Pedro Schwartz
Research Monograph 58; ISBN 0 255 36535 7
£12.50

The Way Out of the Pensions Quagmire

Philip Booth & Deborah Cooper

Research Monograph 60; ISBN 0 255 36517 9

£12.50

Black Wednesday

A Re-examination of Britain's Experience in the Exchange Rate Mechanism

Alan Budd

Occasional Paper 135; ISBN 0 255 36566 7

£7.50

Crime: Economic Incentives and Social Networks

Paul Ormerod

Hobart Paper 151; ISBN 0 255 36554 3

£10.00

The Road to Serfdom *with* The Intellectuals and Socialism

Friedrich A. Hayek

Occasional Paper 136; ISBN 0 255 36576 4

£10.00

To order copies of currently available IEA papers, or to enquire about availability, please contact:

Lavis Marketing
IEA orders
FREEPOST LON21280
Oxford OX3 7BR

Tel: 01865 767575
Fax: 01865 750079
Email: orders@lavismarketing.co.uk

The IEA also offers a subscription service to its publications. For a single annual payment, currently £40.00 in the UK, you will receive every title the IEA publishes during the course of a year, invitations to events, and discounts on our extensive back catalogue. For more information, please contact:

Adam Myers
Subscriptions
The Institute of Economic Affairs
2 Lord North Street
London SW1P 3LB

Tel: 020 7799 8920
Fax: 020 7799 2137
Website: www.iea.org.uk